John Keats, Johannes Hoops

Hyperion

John Keats, Johannes Hoops

Hyperion

ISBN/EAN: 9783743351097

Hergestellt in Europa, USA, Kanada, Australien, Japan

Cover: Foto ©ninafisch / pixelio.de

Manufactured and distributed by brebook publishing software (www.brebook.com)

John Keats, Johannes Hoops

Hyperion

Englische Textbibliothek
Herausgegeben von
Johannes Hoops
a. o. Professor an der Universität Heidelberg

3.

KEATS'
HYPERION

Mit Einleitung herausgegeben
von
Johannes Hoops

> His fragment of 'Hyperion'
> seems actually inspired by the
> Titans, and is as sublime as
> Aeschylus. Byron.

HEIDELBERG
Carl Winter's Universitätsbuchhandlung

Alle Rechte vorbehalten.

Druck von Emil Felber in Weimar.

Inhalt.

	Seite
Einleitung	1
I. Entstehungsgeschichte	3
II. Urteil der Zeitgenossen und der Nachwelt	10
III. Litterarhistorische Stellung	16
IV. Die Ueberarbeitung des *Hyperion* als Vision	27
V. Bibliographisches	38
1. *Hyperion*	38
2. *Vision*	42
3. Die vorliegende Ausgabe	43
Hyperion. A Fragment	47
Hyperion, a Vision	83

Einleitung.

Keats, Hyperion.

1. Entstehungsgeschichte.

Während Keats noch am *Endymion* arbeitete, im Jahre 1817, trug er sich bereits mit einem neuen poetischen Plan aus dem Gebiet der klassischen Mythologie: der Mondromanze *Endymion* sollte eine Sonnenromanze *Hyperion* an die Seite gestellt werden. "Thy lute-voic'd brother will I sing ere long" ruft er dem Liebling Dianens zu (End. 4. 774), und die Vorrede des *Endymion* schliesst er am 10. April 1818 mit den Worten: „Ich hoffe, ich habe nicht in zu später Stunde Griechenlands schöne Mythologie behandelt und ihren Glanz nicht getrübt: denn ich möchte mich noch einmal daran versuchen[1], bevor ich von ihr Abschied nehme." In einem Briefe an seinen Bruder George endlich sagt er direkt, dass er schon vor des ersteren Abreise aus England, also im Frühling 1818, als Thema seiner nächsten Dichtung den „Sturz des Hyperion" im Auge hatte[2].

---

[1] Woodhouse bestätigt ausdrücklich, dass Keats hiermit den *Hyperion* meinte. Vgl. KW. 2, 113, a. 1. (KW. bezeichnet Buxton Forman's vierbändige Gesamtausgabe von Keat's Werken. London, Reeves & Turner. 1883. Zweite, vermehrte und verbesserte Aufl. 1889.)

[2] "I think you knew before you left England, that my next subject would be the fall of Hyperion." Die Worte sind um Weihnachten 1818 geschrieben. Vgl. The Letters of John Keats. Complete revised edition etc. Edited by H. Buxton Forman. London, Reeves & Turner. 1895. S. 243. (Weiterhin citiert als Lett. ed. Form.)

Nach Veröffentlichung des *Endymion* wandte er sich zunächst freilich einem ganz andersartigen Stoffe zu, der romantischen Dichtung *Isabella*, die im April und Mai 1818 entstand. Und in den Sommermonaten desselben Jahres kam er überhaupt kaum zu zusammenhängendem poetischem Schaffen. Im Juni heiratete sein Bruder George, um gleich darauf mit seiner jungen Frau nach Amerika auszuwandern. Keats und sein Freund Brown gaben ihnen bis Liverpool das Geleit und traten von da aus eine mehrwöchentliche Erholungsreise durch Schottland an, auf welcher der Dichter durch überanstrengende Fussmärsche bei regnerischem Wetter den Grund zu jener tückischen Krankheit legte, die ihn so vorzeitig dahinraffen sollte. Als er am 18. August nach Hause zurückkehrte, fand er seinen Bruder Tom sterbenskrank. Selbst leidend, hat er ihn dann in nie ermattender Hingabe treu bis zum Tode gepflegt. Und zu diesem häuslichen Leiden kamen gleichzeitig im August und September 1818 jene hämischen Rezensionen seines *Endymion* in *Blackwood's Magazine* und der *Quarterly Review*, die gewiss dazu angethan waren, den Stolz eines aufstrebenden Dichtergeistes aufs tiefste zu verletzen, wenngleich ihre Wirkung früher zum Teil lächerlich überschätzt worden ist.

Es scheint wohl, dass Keats unter dem unmittelbaren Eindruck jener Kritiken in augenblicklicher Erregung seinen Freunden erklärt hat, er werde nie wieder eine Zeile schreiben. Wie wenig Ernst es ihm damit war, sagt er selbst in einem Briefe vom 27. Oktober 1818 (KW. 3,233 f.). Die Worte eines Dichters, meint er, müsse man nicht auf die Goldwage legen; ein Dichter sei von Haus aus charakterlos, eine Chamäleonnatur, die bald so, bald so empfinde. „Und wenn ich ein Dichter bin, was Wunder, dass ich sage, ich wolle nicht mehr schreiben? Konnte ich nicht in demselben

Augenblick über die Charaktere von Saturn und Ops nachdenken?"

Auch aus andern Briefen dieser Zeit ergiebt sich, dass er von den bangen Sorgen und aufreibenden Mühen der Krankenpflege in der Poesie fieberhaft Erholung suchte. „Ich muss schreiben und mich in abstrakte Bilder stürzen", bemerkt er in seinem Brief vom 21. September an Dilke (KW. 3,225), um mich von seinem Aussehen, seiner Stimme und Schwäche zu erholen, so dass ich jetzt in beständigem Fieber lebe." „Es muss Gift für das Leben sein, obgleich ich mich wohl fühle", fügt er ahnungsvoll hinzu. Auch in einem Brief an Reynolds vom gleichen oder folgenden Tage spricht er von der „fieberhaften Erholung der Poesie" und weiter, ähnlich wie oben: „Ich bin in jene Abstraktionen zurück verfallen, welche mein einziges Leben sind" (KW. 3,228).

So sehen wir ihn inmitten all der Prüfungen und Leiden aufs neue poetisch thätig: unter den Anfeindungen einer gehässigen Parteikritik, am Krankenbette seines Bruders entwirft er das Werk, das viele für sein grösstes halten, den *Hyperion*. Kann es ein sprechenderes Zeugnis geben für den unbeugsamen, mannhaften Geist, den siegesbewussten Dichterstolz, der in diesem verspotteten „Apothekerlehrling" lebte?

Freilich wird Keats, solange er den Bruder zu pflegen hatte, über die ersten Entwürfe zu der neuen Dichtung schwerlich hinausgekommen sein. Ein zusammenhängendes poetisches Schaffen war unter solchen Umständen kaum möglich. In einem Brief vom 20. Oktober spricht er dies selber aus[1]. Umso hastiger stürzte er sich nach Toms

---

[1] „In the way I am at present situated I have too many interruptions to a train of feeling to be able to write Poetry" (KW. 3, S. XLIV. Letters ed. Forman 222).

Tode (Anfang Dezember 1818) in die Arbeit, schon um seinen Schmerz zu betäuben. „Ich habe ein neues Blatt anzufangen", schreibt er am 18. Dezember 1818; „ich muss arbeiten; ich muss lesen; ich muss schreiben" (KW. 3,248).

Und jetzt beginnt eine wunderbare Periode poetischen Schaffens, die ihres Gleichen sucht in der Geschichte der Weltlitteratur. Im Laufe weniger Monate entstanden jene Meisterschöpfungen, welche Keats mit einem Schlage in die Reihe der ersten englischen Dichter rückten und später seinen tiefgreifenden Einfluss auf die Poesie und Malerei der Victorianischen Epoche begründeten.

Aber gleichzeitig geriet er in den Bannkreis eines Magneten, der ihn nicht mehr los liess und fortan seinem ganzen Denken und Empfinden eine neue Richtung gab. Wie unvermischter Sauerstoff die Lebensthätigkeit des Körpers aufs äusserste belebt, zugleich aber die Auflösung der Organe beschleunigt, so hat die Leidenschaft zu Fanny Brawne erst nicht unwesentlich zur Steigerung von Keats' poetischer Schaffenskraft beigetragen, um schliesslich mit tötlich versengender Glut sein Lebensmark vorzeitig zu verzehren. Die Abfassung des *Hyperion* fällt in die aufsteigende Bahn dieser Leidenschaft, die Ueberarbeitung desselben in die Form einer *Vision* in die absteigende.

Bald nach Toms Tode, noch im Dezember 1818, war Keats auf die Einladung seines Freundes Brown in dessen Haus, Wentworth Place in Hampstead, übergesiedelt. „It was then he wrote *Hyperion*", sagt Brown mit Bezug auf die ersten Wochen ihres Zusammenlebens[1]). Die eigentliche Ausarbeitung des Gedichtes, das ihn am Krankenlager Toms schon so lebhaft beschäftigte, wurde offenbar

---

[1]) Colvin, Keats (Engl. Men of Letters) S. 228.

erst jetzt in Angriff genommen [1]). Zwei Aeusserungen in dem langen Tagebuchbrief des Dichters an seine Verwandten in Amerika bestätigen uns dies. An der ersten, schon einmal kurz berührten Stelle heisst es: „Ich meine, Ihr wusstet, bevor Ihr England verliesst, dass mein nächstes Thema „der Sturz des Hyperion" sein würde. Ich bin gestern abend etwas weiter damit gekommen, aber es wird einige Zeit dauern, bis ich wieder ins richtige Fahrwasser gelange. Ich will Euch [keine Auszüge mitteilen, weil ich möchte, dass das Ganze auf Euch wirkt" (Weihnachten 1818). Und einige Tage später: „Ich will keine Auszüge von meinem grossen Gedicht geben, welches kaum begonnen ist" (Lett. ed. Forman 243. 249).

Im Dezember und in der ersten Hälfte des Januar scheint er vorwiegend am *Hyperion* gearbeitet zu haben. Gleichzeitig freilich reiften in seinem Geiste schon wieder neue Entwürfe, Werke von andersartiger Natur. Im Januar 1819 entstanden die romantischen Dichtungen *Eve of St. Agnes* und *Eve of St. Mark*, die eine so völlig heterogene Saite anschlugen. Es kamen wohl auch Zeiten, wo er die Leier ganz beiseite legte. „Ich bin mit *Hyperion* nicht weiter gekommen", schreibt er am 14. Februar; „denn um die Wahrheit zu sagen, ich bin in letzter Zeit nicht in besonderer Verfassung zum Dichten gewesen. Ich muss warten, bis der Frühling mich etwas aufrüttelt" (Lett. ed. Form. 286).

Und der Frühling brachte ihm die erhoffte Anregung. In der Zeit vom März bis Mai 1819 wurde die Mehrzahl der klassischen *Oden* und *La Belle Dame sans Merci* gedichtet.

---

[1]) In dieser Beziehung hat Forman (KW. 2, 143) Colvin gegenüber recht. Anderseits ist es nach den früher angeführten Belegen sicher, dass Entwürfe zu der Dichtung schon an Toms Sterbelager gemacht wurden.

Damals scheint er auch den *Hyperion* soweit fertiggestellt zu haben, wie er uns heute vorliegt. Woodhouse, ein Freund des Dichters, der das Manuskript im April 1819 las, sagt, es habe damals $2\frac{1}{2}$ Bücher mit im ganzen etwa 900 Versen umfasst. Eine Abschrift, die Woodhouse im Sommer 1819 anfertigte, enthält 892 Verse und ein Wort[1]). Da das Gedicht in der veröffentlichten Fassung 883 Verse und ein Wort zählt, so hat Keats also nach dem April 1819 nichts weiter hinzugefügt. Er war, wie Woodhouse berichtet, schon damals unzufrieden mit dem, was er geschrieben, und sagte, er werde es nicht beenden. In den Sommermonaten war er jedenfalls mit der Abfassung von *Otho the Great*, *Lamia* und *King Stephen* vollauf beschäftigt[2]). Doch scheint er im Spätsommer 1819 während seines Aufenthaltes zu Winchester, der letzten glücklichen Zeit seines Lebens, den *Hyperion* aufs neue vorgenommen zu haben. Er feilte hie und da an dem früher Geschriebenen, aber die Arbeit befriedigte ihn jetzt nicht mehr. Am 22. September 1819 schreibt er an Reynolds: „Ich habe *Hyperion* aufgegeben — es waren zu viele Miltonische Inversionen darin"[3]). Damit war die ursprüngliche Fassung endgültig fallen gelassen.

Zu Winchester beendete Keats *Lamia* und dichtete die *Ode auf den Herbst* (September 1819) — seine letzten bedeutenden Schöpfungen. Anfang Oktober kehrte er nach London zurück mit dem Entschluss, sich als Journalist

---

[1]) Vgl. unten Kap. V, 1.

[2]) Wenn er im August 1819 in einem Briefe an Bailey bemerkt: „Ich habe auch Teile meines *Hyperion* geschrieben", so erklärt sich dies daraus, dass er ein ganzes Jahr nicht mit Bailey korrespondiert hatte. Im gleichen Zusammenhang erwähnt er auch *Isabella* und *St. Agnes' Eve*. Vgl. Colvin, Keats 229.

[3]) Lett. ed. Form. 380. Weiteres über die Ursachen dieses Entschlusses s. im 4. Kapitel.

seinen Weg durchs Leben zu erkämpfen. Er bezog zu
diesem Zweck eine Wohnung in Westminster. Aber schon
zwei Tage nach seiner Rückkehr trieb es ihn nach Hampstead
hinaus zu der Geliebten, die er seit vier Monaten
nicht gesprochen hatte. Von dem Augenblick, wo er sie
wieder sah, flammte die alte Leidenschaft, die in der Entfernung
geschlummert, heftiger denn je empor. Phantasie
und Gefühl gewannen wieder die Herrschaft über den
Willen. Alle Gedanken an einen praktischen Broterwerb
wurden in den Wind geschlagen, die Wohnung in Westminster
aufgegeben, und kaum vierzehn Tage nach der
Rückkehr aus Winchester finden wir ihn bereits wieder mit
seinem Freunde Brown zusammen wohnen, um der Geliebten
möglichst nahe zu sein. Es ist das Bild des Falters,
der in die Flamme fliegt. Keats selbst wusste genau, dass
dies der Anfang vom Ende sei. „Ich werde nichts thun
können", schreibt er ahnungsvoll, „Ich möchte den Würfel
werfen für Liebe oder Tod. Ich habe keine Geduld für
irgend etwas anderes" (Lett. ed. Form. 433).

Das war keine normale Gemütsverfassung mehr, keine
Stimmung, aus der etwas Vollendetes entspringen konnte.
Aber poetisch thätig war er auch jetzt. Nach einem misslungenen
Versuche, den *Otho* auf die Bühne zu bringen,
begann er ein satirisches Feengedicht, *The Cap and Bells*,
an dem er allmorgenlich arbeitete. Und gleichzeitig nahm
er sein Lieblingsthema, den *Hyperion*, wieder auf. „An den
Abenden", schreibt Brown, „sass er auf seinen Wunsch in
einem Zimmer für sich und war eifrig beschäftigt, das
Fragment *Hyperion* in die Form einer Vision umzuarbeiten"
(Colvin, Keats 185). So entstand im Spätjahr 1819 jene
seltsame Schöpfung *Hyperion, a Vision*, die erst lange nach
des Dichters Tode bekannt und früher fälschlich für einen
ersten Entwurf der Dichtung gehalten wurde[1].

---

[1] Von Colvin (Keats 230 ff.) mit schlagenden Gründen widerlegt.
Vgl. auch Forman KW. 2, 143 f.

In der Einleitung derselben erhebt sich die Phantasie des Dichters stellenweise noch wieder zu der alten Höhe; aber als Ganzes hält diese Umarbeitung einen Vergleich mit der veröffentlichten Fassung nicht aus. Wir verdanken es dem eindringlichen Rat seiner Freunde, wenn Keats sich entschloss, nicht die *Vision*, sondern die erste Fassung, obwohl sie für ihn einen überwundenen Standpunkt bedeutete, der Oeffentlichkeit zu übergeben (Colvin, Keats 196).

„*Hyperion, A Fragment*" erschien in der ersten Juliwoche 1820 in dem dritten und letzten Bande seiner Gedichte, der betitelt war: „*Lamia, Isabella, The Eve of St. Agnes, and other Poems.* By John Keats, Author of Endymion. London: Printed for Taylor and Hessey, Fleet-Street. 1820". In einem Vorwort zu dem Bande bemerkten die Verleger, sie allein seien für die Veröffentlichung dieses Fragments verantwortlich, „da es auf ihre besondere Bitte und gegen den Wunsch des Verfassers gedruckt" sei. Das Gedicht habe ebenso lang wie *Endymion* werden sollen, aber wegen der schlechten Aufnahme des letzteren habe der Dichter die Fortsetzung aufgegeben — eine Behauptung, die wohl mehr auf buchhändlerischer Effekthascherei als auf Thatsachen beruhte.

Hyperion, a Vision wurde erst 35 Jahre nach des Dichters Tode von seinem Biographen Monckton Milnes in den *Miscellanies of the Philobiblon Society* (vol. III, 1856—57) veröffentlicht.

II. Urteil der Zeitgenossen und der Nachwelt.

Wie Keats' Freunde über das Fragment *Hyperion* dachten, möge das Urteil von Woodhouse und Hunt zeigen. Woodhouse sagt: „Der Bau der Dichtung sowohl wie der Gegenstand ist kolossal. Es schwebt ein Zug von ruhiger Erhabenheit darüber, welche das Zeichen wahrer Kraft ist.

Ich wüsste kein Gedicht, mit dem es in dieser Hinsicht verglichen werden könnte. Es ist dasselbe in der Poesie, was die Elgin- und ägyptischen Marmorbilder in der Skulptur sind" (KW. 2, 144).

Leigh Hunt, der den Band von 1820 in seinem *Indicator* vom 2. und 9. August 1820 ausführlich besprach, äussert sich über *Hyperion* folgendermassen: „Der *Hyperion* ist ein Fragment, — ein gigantisches, wie eine Ruine in der Wüste oder die Gebeine des Mastodon. Er ist wirklich mit seinem Stoff aus dem gleichen Stück"[1]). Und in seinen Erinnerungen an Keats in *Lord Byron and some of his Contemporaries* sagt er von *Hyperion*, er sei „wie das Bruchstück einer früheren Welt". „Es ist eine Sprache darin, erhabener als irgend eine, die in unsern Tagen geredet worden ist, ausser in einigen von Wordsworths Sonetten" (KW. 4, 290).

Jeffrey, der bekannte schottische Kritiker, der in der *Edinburgh Review* vom 20. August 1820 den *Endymion* und den Band von 1820 zusammen einer im ganzen recht günstigen Kritik unterzog, glaubt doch von einer Vollendung des *Hyperion* abraten zu sollen. „Denn obgleich Stellen von einiger Kraft und Erhabenheit darin sind, so zeigt die uns vorliegende Probe doch klar genug, dass der Stoff zu weit von allen Quellen menschlichen Interesses entfernt ist, um von einem modernen Dichter erfolgreich behandelt zu werden" (KW. 1, 366).

Es ist eine merkwürdige Ironie des Schicksals, dass gerade dasjenige Werk, das Keats selbst am wenigsten befriedigte, seinen Ruhm über den engen Kreis seiner Londoner Freunde hinaustrug. Es war infolge dessen auch das erste, das die Augen des Auslands auf sich lenkte.

Crabbe Robinson, der Freund des Weimarer Dichter-

---

[1]) KW. 2, 536, wo die ganze Rezension abgedruckt ist.

kreises, schrieb 1820 in sein Tagebuch: „Ich habe den Aders etwas von Keats' Gedichten vorgelesen, den Anfang von *Hyperion* wirklich ein viel versprechendes Stück. Es ist eine Kraft, Wildheit und Originalität in den Werken dieses jungen Dichters, die, wenn seine gefährliche Reise nach Italien ihn nicht zerstört, versprechen, ihn an die Spitze der nächsten Dichtergeneration zu stellen. Lamb stellt ihn gleich hinter Wordsworth — ohne damit einen Vergleich zu beabsichtigen, denn sie sind einander unähnlich"[1]).

Auch Shelley war voll Bewunderung für das Werk. In seinem unvollendeten Brief an den Herausgeber der *Quarterly Review* empfiehlt er den *Hyperion* dessen besonderer Beachtung. „Der grösste Teil dieser Dichtung ist sicherlich in dem alleredelsten poetischen Stil geschrieben. Ich spreche unparteiisch, denn die Geschmacksregeln, denen Keats in seinen andern Dichtungen gefolgt ist, sind das gerade Gegenteil von meinen eignen." Der Brief wurde bald nach Empfang des *Lamia*-Bandes geschrieben, aber niemals abgeschickt[2]). Offenbar gleichzeitig hiermit, Anfang November 1820, schrieb Shelley aus Pisa an Peacock: „Unter den neuen Sachen, die mich erreicht haben, ist ein Band Gedichte von Keats; in anderer Hinsicht unbedeutend genug, aber er enthält das Fragment eines Gedichtes *Hyperion*. Sie haben vielleicht nicht Zeit, es zu lesen; aber es ist sicher eine bewunderungswürdige Dichtung und giebt mir eine Meinung von Keats, die ich offen gestanden früher nicht hatte" (KW. 4, 248). In einem Brief an Frau Hunt vom 11. November 1820 drückt er sich ähnlich aus: „Keats' neuer Band ist bei uns eingetroffen, und das Fragment

---

[1]) Abgedruckt von W. T. Arnold in der Einleitung zu seiner Sonderausgabe von *Hyperion*, Buch I, S. 5.

[2]) Er findet sich bei Forman KW. 3, 384 ff. abgedruckt.

Hyperion lässt von ihm hoffen, dass er bestimmt ist, einer der ersten Dichter unseres Zeitalters zu werden." In demselben Briefe erkundigt er sich mit Besorgnis: „Wo ist Keats jetzt? Ich erwarte ihn mit Spannung in Italien, wo ich ihm dann angelegentlich jede mögliche Aufmerksamkeit erweisen werde. Ich halte sein Leben für sehr wertvoll, und ich nehme innigen Anteil an seinem Wohlergehen. Ich will der Arzt seines Körpers und seiner Seele sein, den einen warm halten und die andere Griechisch und Spanisch lehren. Ich bin mir teilweise wohl bewusst, dass ich einen Rivalen pflege, der mich weit übertreffen wird; und das ist ein Grund mehr und wird meine Freude erhöhen" (KW. 4, 249 f.). Diese Bewunderung für *Hyperion* war bei Shelley nicht blos vorübergehend. Drei Monate später (am 15. Febr. 1821) schreibt er abermals an Peacock: „Schliessen Sie in Ihre Bannflüche gegen die modernen Versuche in der Poesie auch Keats' *Hyperion* ein? Ich finde ihn sehr schön. Seine andern Gedichte sind wenig wert; aber wenn der *Hyperion* keine erhabene Poesie ist, so ist von unsern Zeitgenossen überhaupt keine geschrieben worden" (KW. 4, 250). Und im Eingang der Vorrede zum *Adonais*, diesem unsterblichen Freundesdenkmal für den zu früh verstorbenen Dichter, dessen Name nach seiner eignen Meinung „in Wasser geschrieben war", spricht sich Shelley ebenso entschieden aus. „Es ist meine Absicht, der Londoner Ausgabe dieses Gedichtes eine Kritik der Ansprüche anzufügen, die der betrauerte Held desselben auf einen Platz unter den genialsten Schriftstellern unsers Zeitalters hat. Meine bekannte Abneigung gegen die engen Geschmacksregeln, nach denen verschiedene seiner früheren Schöpfungen geformt waren, beweisen wenigstens, dass ich ein unparteiischer Richter bin. Ich halte das Fragment *Hyperion* für so bedeutend wie irgend etwas, was jemals von einem Dichter im gleichen Alter geschaffen worden ist." Als Shelley's Leichnam nach jener verhängnisvollen Segelfahrt ans Ufer getrieben wurde, fand man in seiner Tasche ein aufgeschlagenes Buch. Das Letzte, was der Sänger des *Adonais* auf Erden gelesen hatte, war der *Hyperion* des von ihm verherrlichten Keats, der ihm in die Ewigkeit voraufgegangen war.

Nicht minder anerkennend — wie Shelley äusserte sich Byron über die Dichtung. Wenige Monate nach Keats' Tode, am 30. Juli 1821, bemerkte er in einem Briefe an Murray: „Sein *Hyperion* ist ein schönes Denkmal und wird seinen Namen bewahren" (KW. 4,269). Und nicht lange nachher schreibt er: „Meine Entrüstung über Keats' Feindseligkeit gegen Pope hat mich kaum seinem eignen Genie gerecht werden lassen, welches trotz all der phantastischen Narrheiten seines Stils zweifellos vielversprechend war. Sein Fragment *Hyperion* scheint wirklich von den Titanen inspiriert und ist so erhaben wie Aeschylus" (KW. 4.270).

Dieses günstige Urteil der grössten unter den Zeitgenossen ist in der Hauptsache auch von der Nachwelt bis heute geteilt worden. Drei Aeusserungen aus der zweiten Hälfte des Jahrhunderts mögen dies beweisen.

Swinburne, der Dichter und Kritiker, meint: „Der Triumph des *Hyperion* ist beinahe so vollkommen wie der Misserfolg des *Endymion*"[1]). Sidney Colvin fasst sein Urteil dahin zusammen: „Mit ein paar Fehlern und Ungleichheiten und ein oder zwei Fällen von Unkorrektheit im Ausdruck ist *Hyperion*, soweit er uns vorliegt, in der That eines der grossartigsten Gedichte in unserer Sprache, und in seiner Grossartigkeit scheint es zugleich eins der leichtesten und spontansten zu sein" (a. a. O. 157). Georg Brandes endlich schreibt in seinen *Hauptströmungen der Litteratur des*

---

[1]) In der *Encyclop. Brit.* Wieder abgedruckt in den *Miscellanies*. London 1886. S. 214.

neunzehnten Jahrhunderts (4,232), nachdem er auf die Schönheiten der Oden und früheren Gedichte hingewiesen hat: „Allein erst in den wenigen fertig gewordenen Gesängen des *Hyperion* gelang es Keats, seine Kunstmittel völlig zu beherrschen und das Ideal plastisch-sinnlicher Bestimmtheit, welches ihm vorschwebte, zu verwirklichen. Hier ist das Relief verschwunden, um der Statue Platz zu machen, und Statuen von einem Stile, als habe der Meissel Michel Angelos bei ihrer Hervorbringung mitgewirkt. Mag man das Studium Miltons heraushühlen, ich bekenne, dass für mich Milton hier übertroffen ist."

Man wird sich diesen enthusiastischen Urteilen im grossen und ganzen unbedenklich anschliessen dürfen. Auch uns erscheint *Hyperion* als eine der erhabensten Schöpfungen der neueren englischen Poesie. Aber bei aller Anerkennung für die Grossartigkeit der Dichtung darf man doch nicht vergessen, dass sie nur ein gigantisches Bruchstück ist, an dem man die klassische Durcharbeitung der Einzelheiten bewundern, von dessen vollendeter Gestalt man sich aber keine Vorstellung machen kann. Es ist eine Frage, ob das Stück bei seiner grossartigen Anlage eine Fortsetzung vertragen hätte. Das einzige vollendete Werk des Dichters, das sich etwa vergleichen liesse, der *Endymion*, spricht nicht gerade dafür. Schon in dieser Romanze tritt der Mangel an Handlung fühlbar zu Tage: wie viel stärker hätte er sich bei einem Epos geltend machen müssen, das auf zehn Bücher angelegt war, und bei dem die Ueberlieferung eine äusserst spärliche Grundlage für den Aufbau der Fabel bot! Ueberdies haben derartige Stoffe aus der antiken Mythenwelt, wie Jeffrey mit Recht hervorhebt, überhaupt zu wenig individuelles menschliches Interesse, um als Gegenstand umfangreicher Dichtungen moderne Leser zu fesseln.

Auch über den Rang, der dem *Hyperion* unter den Schöpfungen des Dichters gebührt, wird man heute wohl etwas anders urteilen als vor achtzig Jahren. Von den Darstellungen aus der antiken Welt ist *Hyperion* allerdings die grossartigste, erhabenste, aber *Lamia* übertrifft ihn durch die berückende Schönheit von Sprache und Vers und die harmonische Vollendung des Ganzen. Und zieht man auch die romantischen Dichtungen zum Vergleich heran, so werden die meisten heutigen Leser doch wohl dem unübertrefflichen *Eve of St. Agnes* die Palme zuerkennen. Auf jeden Fall haben die romantischen Meisterwerke ungleich tiefere Spuren in der Victorianischen Litteratur hinterlassen als der von den Zeitgenossen am höchsten geschätzte *Hyperion*.

III. Litterarhistorische Stellung.

Aber welchen Rang der individuelle Geschmack dem *Hyperion* immer zuteilen mag: dass er einen gewaltigen Fortschritt gegenüber *Endymion* bezeichnet, obwohl nur ein Jahr die beiden trennt, wird niemand leugnen. Im *Endymion* suchte Keats, zum Teil noch unter dem Einfluss Leigh Hunts, im Gegensatz zu der konventionellen Korrektheit der Popeschen Schule sein Vorbild in der genialen Regellosigkeit der Elisabethaner. Die Dichtung enthält eine Menge origineller Gedanken und liefert Beweise genug für die poetische Schöpferkraft des Verfassers; aber sie entbehrt des ruhigen Gleichmasses, die Einzelschilderung überwuchert, der Dichter lässt seine Phantasie schrankenlos schalten, giebt allen seinen Einfällen Raum, und so kommt es, dass unter dem üppig emporschiessenden Rankenwerk poetischer Bilder und Vergleiche der Faden der Erzählung den Blicken nicht selten verhüllt wird. Hin und wieder finden sich wohl Stellen voll antiker Grösse, wie der Hymnus auf Pan und das Lied der Bacchantin, aber im allgemeinen ist *Endymion* von der ruhigen, harmonischen Schönheit klassischer Werke weit entfernt.

Der Dichter fühlte das wohl selbst. Er suchte nach einem besseren Wegweiser zum Geist des Altertums und fand ihn in dem Sänger des *Paradise Lost*, der ja auch den Deutschen einer der ersten Vermittler antiker Kultur gewesen war. Keats war schon lange mit seinen Dichtungen vertraut. Cowden Clarke, dem er die Bekanntschaft mit Spenser verdankte, hatte ihn auch in die Werke Miltons eingeführt[1]). Die *Ode an Apollo* (Febr. 1815) zeugt bereits von verständnisvoller Bewunderung für „Milton's tuneful thunders", bei deren Schall die Himmel lauschen. Auch in andern Jugenddichtungen finden sich Anklänge an Milton. Im allgemeinen aber scheint den jungen Dichter mehr die mildere Schönheit des *Comus*, *Lycidas*, *Allegro* und *Penseroso* als die grossartige Erhabenheit des *Paradise Lost* gefesselt zu haben.

Nach der Vollendung des *Endymion* nun, als gerade der Plan zu dem Sturz des Hyperion im Geist des Dichters bestimmtere Formen anzunehmen begann, setzt ein erneutes und eindringenderes Studium Miltons ein. Schon am 21. Januar 1818 begeisterte ihn eine Locke des blinden Barden, die er bei Leigh Hunt sah, zu den bewunderungsvollen *Lines on seeing a Lock of Milton's Hair*. Eine humorvolle Epistel an James Rice vom 25. März 1818 (KW. 3,135) legt von seiner Beschäftigung mit Milton Zeugnis ab, und einen Monat später, am 27. April, schreibt er an Reynolds ausdrücklich: „Ich trage Verlangen, mich am alten Homer zu laben, wie wir's an Shakespeare thaten, und wie ich mich in letzter Zeit an Milton gelabt habe"

---

[1]) In seiner *Epistel an Cowden Clarke* (Sept. 1816) spricht der Dichter dies selber aus:

„You first taught me all the sweets of song: . . . .
Spenserian vowels that elope with ease, ...
Miltonian storms, and more, Miltonian tenderness."

(KW. 3,146). Im nächsten Briefe an denselben Freund (vom 3. Mai 1818) zieht er einen ausführlichen Vergleich zwischen dem poetischen Genie Miltons und Wordsworths. Aus dem Jahr 1818 oder 1819 stammen ferner die wichtigen Glossen zum *Verlornen Paradies*[1]), die besser als alles andere erkennen lassen, wie genau er dieses Epos gelesen hatte. Und noch im August 1819 schreibt er von Winchester aus: „Shakespeare und das *Verlorne Paradies* werden jeden Tag grössere Wunder für mich". Aehnlich wenige Tage später noch einmal: „Ich werde jeden Tag mehr überzeugt, dass schön Schreiben (fine writing) nächst schön Handeln das Beste in der Welt ist; das *Verlorne Paradies* wird ein grösseres Wunder"[2]).

Ob das Studium des *Paradise Lost* vielleicht eine direkte Folge seiner Beschäftigung mit dem Entwurf einer Hyperion-Dichtung war, lässt sich nicht sagen. Jedenfalls musste ihn sein Stoff, der Streit um die Herrschaft des Himmels, von selbst an den biblischen Titanenkampf des *Verlornen Paradieses* erinnern. Die Lektüre des letzteren aber ist ihrerseits von der grössten Bedeutung für die Gestaltung des *Hyperion* geworden.

Die Dichtung war ursprünglich als Romanze von der Länge des *Endymion* geplant. Die Grossartigkeit des gewaltigen Stoffs und das Vorbild Miltons veranlassten den Dichter, ein Epos daraus zu machen, welches zehn Bücher umfassen sollte. Statt des heroischen Reimpaars, des Lieblingsmetrums Leigh Hunts, das Keats im *Endymion* und später wieder in der *Lamia* anwandte, wurde nach dem Muster des *Paradise Lost* der Blankvers gewählt. Es war das erste Mal, dass Keats in diesem Versmass dichtete; umso bewunderungswürdiger ist die Meisterschaft, mit der er es handhabt.

---
[1]) Abgedruckt von Forman KW. 3. 19.
[2]) Lett. ed. Form. 364. 369.

Einleitung.

Auch in den **Charakteren und Szenen** des *Hyperion* finden sich manche Anklänge aus *Verlorne Paradies*, die sich allerdings zum Teil durch die Aehnlichkeit des Stoffs erklären. Hier wie dort haben wir ein Titanengeschlecht, das durch eine überlegene göttliche Macht aus dem Himmel in die Unterwelt gestürzt ist und nun auf Rache sinnt. Dem Rat der Teufel im zweiten Buch des *Verlornen Paradieses* entspricht die Titanenversammlung im zweiten Gesang des *Hyperion*. Saturn und Satan, Oceanus und Belial, Enceladus und Moloch sind Parallelen, die sich von selbst aufdrängen.

Die bedeutende Einwirkung Miltons auf Keats' **Wortschatz und Sprachgebrauch** ist schon durch W. T. Arnold in der trefflichen Einleitung zu seiner Ausgabe der Dichtungen[1]) gewürdigt worden. Seine Zusammenstellungen lassen sich leicht vermehren. Verschiedene seltnere Wörter sind augenscheinlich auf die Lektüre Miltons zurückzuführen. Dazu gehören im *Hyperion*:

argent: Hyp. 1. 284 two fair argent wings (von der Sonne, dafür v. 296 silver wings). Vgl. Milton P. L. 3, 460 those argent fields (vom Mond).

colure: 1, 274 broad-belting c. Vgl. P. L. 9, 66 From pole to pole, traversing each colure. S. Arnolds Note in s. Separ. Ausg. Die ganze Stelle ist nach dem Muster der astronomischen Schilderungen im P. L. geschaffen.

essence: 1. 232. 2. 331. 3. 104. Bei Milton öfter: P. L. 1, 425. 2, 215. 3, 6. 9, 166. Com. 462. Circumcis. 7. Braucht aber nicht gerade auf der Lektüre Miltons zu beruhen.

gurge: 2, 28 With sanguine feverous boiling gurge of pulse (von den in der Unterwelt gefesselten Titanen). Die Stelle ist offenbar teilweise eine Reminiscenz aus P. L.

---

[1]) *The Poetical Works of John Keats.* Ed. by W. T. Arnold. London. Kegan Paul, Trench & Co. 1888. Pr. 3 s. 6 d.

12, 41 f. a black bituminous gurge Boils out from under ground, the mouth of Hell.

inlet im ursprünglichen Sinn von Eingang überhaupt: 1, 211. Vgl. Comus 839 through the porch and inlet of each sense. (S. Arnold z. d. St.)

lucent: 1, 239 my l. empire. Arnold vergleicht P. L. 3, 589 in the Sun's lucent orb.

oozy: 2, 170 the God of the Sea ... Arose, with locks not oozy. Reminiszenz aus Lyc. 175 his oozy locks he laves. Vgl. auch Hymn on Christ's Nativ. 124 And bid the weltering waves their oozy channel keep.

orbed: 1, 166 Blazing Hyperion on his orbed fire (von der Sonne). Das Wort begegnet bei Milton P. L. 6, 543 gripe fast his orbed shield. Hymn on Chr. Nat. 143 orbed in a rainbow. Es kommt aber auch sonst vor. z. B. bei Shakespeare, Twelfth Night V, 1 that orbed continent, the fire That severs day from night.

osier: 3, 34 Beside the osiers of a rivulet. Vgl. Comus 890 f. By the rush-yfringed bank. Where grows the willow and the osier dank.

reluctant: 1, 61. Dies Wort hat Keats besonders gut gefallen. In seinen Randglossen zum *Paradise Lost* bemerkt er bei der Stelle 6, 56—58 (Clouds began To darken all the hill, and smoke to roll In dusky wreaths reluctant flames): „*Reluctant* hat durch Vereinigung und Verflechtung seines ursprünglichen und modernen Sinnes, mit all seinen Bedeutungsschattierungen eine kraftvolle Wirkung" (KW. 3, 28). Milton braucht das Wort noch zweimal: PL. 4, 311 sweet, reluctant, amorous delay und 10, 515 down he fell ... Reluctant, but in vain.

slope: 1. 204 Hyperion ... Came slope upon the threshold of the west. Das Wort ist als adj. sehr selten. Arnold zieht zwei Stellen aus Milton heran: P. L. 4, 260 f. Meanwhile murmuring waters fall Down the slope hills und Com. 98 f. And the slope sun his upward beam Shoots against the dusky pole. Ausserdem vgl. P. L. 4, 591 Bore him slope downward to the sun.

sorran: 3, 115. Bei Milton in dieser Schreibung sehr häufig: P. L. 1, 246. 753. 2, 244. 3, 22. 145. 4, 691. 5, 256. 366. 656 und öfter.

unsceptred: 1, 19 His old right hand lay nerveless, listless, dead, Unsceptred. Sceptred kommt bei Milton mehrere Male vor: Pens. 98 In sceptred pall. P. L. 1, 734 Sceptred Angels. 2, 43 Moloch, sc. King. 11, 660 The sc. haralds. Es begegnet aber auch bei Shakespeare.

Mehr noch als in diesen Wortentlehnungen springt Miltons Einfluss in einer bestimmten Art von Wortbildungen ins Auge, worauf Arnold zuerst aufmerksam gemacht hat. Ableitungen von Adjektiven aus Substantiven mittels der Partizipialendung -ed, wie sceptred king, tower'd citadel etc., finden sich wohl bei allen neu-englischen Dichtern und sind in bescheidenem Umfang durchaus einwandfrei. Schon Shakespeare hat eine ziemliche Anzahl solcher Wörter. Durch Milton aber wurde diese Bildungsweise in umfassenderem Masse zur Neuschöpfung poetischer Beiwörter angewandt (s. die Zusammenstellung bei Arnold in der Einleitung zu seiner Ausgabe S. XXXV). Keats geht in der Verwendung dieses Prinzips womöglich noch über Milton hinaus. Im *Hyperion* begegnen an selteneren Wörtern dieser Art: *dungeon'd* 2, 23; *mirror'd* level 1, 257; *mountain'd* world 2, 123; *mouthed* shell, 2, 270; *neighbour'd* 2, 74; *orbed* fire 1, 166; *pedestal'd* (Memphian sphinx) 1, 32; *portion'd* für proportion'd 1, 175; *postured* 1, 85; *unsceptred* (hand) 1, 19. Ferner Komposita: *Black-weeded* pools 1, 230; *calm-throated* (thrush) 3, 38; *far-foamed* sands 2, 172; *green-rob'd* senators 1, 73; *hulk-ear'd* phantoms 1, 230; *lion-thoughted* (Enceladus) 2, 68; *low-ebb'd* (waves) 2, 136; *quick-voic'd* (Thea) 1, 149; *spirit-leaved* book 2, 133; *sweet-shaped* lightnings 1, 276: *tiger-passion'd* (Enceladus) 2, 68. In der *Vision* finden sich: *domed* monument 1, 71; *globed* brain 1, 221; *pedestall'd* (image) 1, 32; *sphered* words 1, 225. Komposita: *happy-noted* voice 1, 164; *sober-pac'd* 1, 93. Diese Bildungen können grösstenteils als gelungene bezeichnet werden. Weniger glücklich und entschuldbar ist es dagegen, wenn Keats solche partizipialen Ableitungen aus Nomina nicht nur als Adjektive, sondern als wirkliche Partizipien gebraucht und mit adverbialen Bestimmungen verbindet. *Bastion'd* wird man sich gefallen lassen, *bastion'd with pyramids* (Hyp. 1, 177) geht über das Erlaubte hinaus. Das Gleiche gilt von Wendungen wie *Space region'd with life-air* Hyp. 1, 119. *slaty ridge Stubborn'd with iron* 2, 17. In dem Falle Tall oaks, *branch-charmed by the earnest stars* 1, 74 kann man zweifeln, ob charmed von dem subst. oder vb. charm abzuleiten ist[1].

Aber neben diesen bestimmt nachweisbaren stofflichen und sprachlichen Anklängen haben wir eine andersartige Einwirkung von seiten Miltons, die minder handgreiflich, aber nicht weniger bedeutungsvoll, weil überall gegenwärtig ist. Im *Paradise Lost* fand Keats ein Muster jenes Masshaltens, jener klassischen Vollendung und Erhabenheit, jener Harmonie von Inhalt und Ausdruck, deren Fehlen *Endymion* den Stempel der Jugendarbeit aufdrückte. Das Streben nach Klarheit und Einfachheit, verbunden mit Strenge der Diktion und Prägnanz und Anschaulichkeit des Ausdrucks, welches den Band von 1820 so hoch über die früheren Versuche des Dichters erhebt und ihm einen bleibenden Platz in der Litteraturgeschichte sichert: dieses Streben ist wohl die wichtigste Frucht der Lektüre des grossen Puritaners gewesen. Man vergleiche nur *Endymion* und

---

[1] Uebrigens hat bei diesen Bildungen ausser Milton sicher auch Chapman auf Keats eingewirkt, der namentlich zusammengesetzte Wörter dieser Art häufig braucht.

Hyperion, und die segensreiche Wirkung desselben wird jedem in die Augen springen.

Im *Hyperion* tritt der Miltonsche Einfluss unzweifelhaft am sichtbarsten zu Tage. Doch ist die Dichtung nichts weniger als eine Nachahmung des *Verlornen Paradieses*. Die sachlichen Aehnlichkeiten ergaben sich, wie wir sahen, zum Teil aus der Verwandtschaft der Stoffe selbst. Die Behandlung von Stil und Versmass im *Hyperion* ist, von den erwähnten Einwirkungen abgesehen, im Grunde doch echt Keatsisch. Milton hätte nie so geschrieben. Die Darstellung ist immer noch zu kompliziert, zu sehr mit modernen Gefühlen und Ideen untermischt, um wirklich klassisch zu sein. Keats hat in dieser Hinsicht sein Vorbild nicht erreicht. Doch ist er antiker und objektiver als Hölderlin, mit dem er oft verglichen wird[1]). Er zeigt überall ein kongeniales Verständnis für den lebendigen Geist der griechischen Mythologie: die Idee des Titanenkampfs insbesondere hat er richtig erfasst. Und die Zuthaten moderner Art gereichen der Dichtung durchaus nicht immer zum Schaden, sie erhöhen vielfach ihren eigentümlichen Reiz. In einigen Punkten anderseits ist Keats Milton entschieden überlegen. So sind namentlich seine Naturschilderungen urwüchsiger als bei Milton, der mehr aus Büchern als aus der Natur schöpft. Auch in den zahlreichen grossartigen Bildern und malenden Beiwörtern, Keats' ureigenster Domäne, ist er Milton mindestens ebenbürtig, wenngleich die Phantasie vielleicht noch zu sehr überwiegt und die Handlung erdrückt. Alles in allem ist *Hyperion* eine Dichtung von völlig originellem Wert und wunderbarer Objektivität. Es ist der erste Ansatz zu einem wirklichen Epos seit Milton, der sich an Erhabenheit der Auffassung und Ausführung mit dem *Verlornen Paradiese* messen kann.

---

[1]) S. Hoops, Engl. Stud. 24, 321.

Neben dem dominierenden Einfluss Miltons treten die Spuren anderer Dichter im *Hyperion* zurück. An zweiter Stelle ist vielleicht Chapman zu nennen, dessen Einwirkung auf Keats auch sonst in mancher Hinsicht diejenige Miltons ergänzt. War er es doch gewesen, dessen Homerübersetzung Keats den ersten Einblick in die Wunderwelt der griechischen Sagen eröffnete (vgl. das Sonett *On first looking into Chapman's Homer*, 1815), der neben Spenser und Leigh Hunt den tiefgreifendsten Einfluss auf seine Jugendpoesie ausübte. Von Chapman hat Keats wahrscheinlich das Verbum *to sphere* entlehnt (Hyp. 1, 117 Open thine eyes eterne, and sphere them round), eins seiner charakteristischen Lieblingswörter, das allerdings auch bei Milton (PL. 7, 247) vorkommt. Auf Chapman's Einfluss beruht zum Teil sicher Keats' Vorliebe für zusammengesetzte Adjektiva, wie branch-charmed (1, 74), broad-belting (1, 274), first-endeavouring (2, 171), softshowering (Vis. 1, 23) u. s. w. Auch die Verwendung des Wortes *proclaim* als Subst. (voices of soft proclaim 1, 130) scheint auf die gleiche Quelle zurückzugehen, da Chapman mehrfach Verba direkt als Substantiva gebraucht (z. B. exclaim, exhort, appall). Mit Chapman und Milton teilt Keats ferner die zahlreiche Verwendung und Neubildung von Adjektiven auf -y, die allerdings gerade im *Hyperion* weniger häufig auftreten: bowery strand (2, 274), pearly seas (1, 355), a serpent's plashy neck (2, 45), scummy marsh (1, 258), slaty ridge (2, 16)[1].

Spensers Einfluss, in den Dichtungen des jungen Keats so bedeutend, ist im *Hyperion* gleich Null. Das Wort *distraught* (1, 232) geht vielleicht auf ihn zurück, obwohl es

---

[1] Vgl. Arnold in seiner Einleitung S. XL. ff. Eine genauere Untersuchung über Chapmans Einfluss auf Keats steht noch aus.

auch bei Shakespeare vorkommt[1]). Die Form *wox* (1, 326) ist wahrscheinlich Spenser entlehnt, der sie sehr häufig verwendet[2]). Zu der heute vulgären Wendung *these like accents* (1, 50) und *such like woe* (1, 159) endlich sei verwiesen auf FQ. 6, 2, 31 (*such like seemly leres*). Das ist aber auch wohl alles.

Shakespeare-Reminiscenzen finden sich an zwei Stellen. Zu den Versen
„Or the familiar visiting of one
Upon the first toll of his passing-bell" (Hyp. 1, 172 f.)
ist zu vergleichen die Stelle in Shakespeares *Macbeth* 1, 5, 46 f.:
„That no compunctious visitings of nature
Shake my fell purpose."

Die Worte:
„Before we knew the winged thing.
Victory, might be lost, or might be won" (Hyp. 2, 341 f.)
erinnern an den bekannten Vers im Hexenlied. *Macbeth* I, 1:
„When the battle is lost and won."

Bemerkenswert ist ferner Keats' Neigung zu willkürlichen Neubildungen. Die Zahl der auf diese Weise von ihm neu geprägten Wörter ist sicher grösser, als Arnold (a. a. O. XLV f.) annimmt, selbst wenn wir von Analogiebildungen nach gegebenen Mustern (wie die Adjektiva auf -ed, -y etc.) absehen. Aus dem *Hyperion* gehören hierher: *aspen-malady* „Schüttelfieber" (Hyp. 1, 94); sonst nirgends belegt. Vgl. Murray New Engl. Dict. 1, 493c, der mit Unrecht aspen als Adjektiv fasst. In der Originalausgabe steht ein Bindestrich.

Aurorian clouds (1, 181). Vgl. Ode to Psyche 20 At tender eye-dawn of aurorean love. Nachgeahmt von Owen

---

[1]) Vgl. Read: *Keats and Spenser*. Heidelberger Doktorschrift. 1897. S. 17 u. 21.

[2]) Ebenda 14.

Meredith („Aurorean clouds") und Swinburne („Aurorean aureole of the sun").

fever out: 1, 138 This passion .. made .. his eyes to fever out. Wahrscheinlich = fieberhaft, krampfhaft hervortreten.

outspreaded: 1, 287 till all outspreaded were. Eine entschieden verunglückte Neubildung.

portion'd statt proportion'd: 1. 175.

realmless: 1, 19 his (Saturn's) realmless eyes were closed. Sonst anscheinend nirgends belegt.

wrinkle in intransitivem Sinne = „sich furchen": This wrinkling brow 1, 100.

Von anderweitigen Einflüssen wären einige Reflexe der schottischen Reise in den Naturschilderungen des *Hyperion* zu erwähnen. Bei dem Verse „Like natural sculpture in cathedral cavern" (1, 86) hat dem Dichter offenbar die Fingalshöhle vorgeschwebt. Schon beim Besuch derselben hatte sich ihm das Bild des Titanenkampfes aufgedrängt. Er schreibt gleich nachher (23. Juli 1818) an Tom: „Denke Dir, die Riesen, die sich gegen Jupiter empörten, hätten eine ganze Masse schwarzer Säulen genommen und sie wie Streichholzbündel zusammengebunden und hätten dann mit ungeheuern Aexten in das Innere dieser Säulen eine Höhle gemacht." Und weiter: „An Feierlichkeit und Grossartigkeit übertrifft sie bei weitem die schönsten Kathedralen" (KW. 3. 201). "This cathedral of the sea" nennt er auch in dem gleichzeitig entstandenen Gedicht *Staffa* die Höhle.

Die berühmte Eingangsszene des *Hyperion* hätte ebenfalls ohne die Eindrücke des schottischen Hochlandes schwerlich jene monumentale Erhabenheit erlangt. Hatte doch der Sohn des Londoner Mietkutschers bis dahin noch gar keine wirklichen Gebirge gesehen! Eine Stelle in einem Brief an Bailey aus Schottland ist in dieser Beziehung interessant genug. „Ich hätte mir diese viermonatliche Fusstour in den Hochlanden nicht gestattet", schreibt der Dichter. „wenn ich nicht gedacht hätte, es würde mir mehr Erfahrung geben, mehr Vorurteile abschleifen, mich an mehr Strapazen gewöhnen, mir schönere Landschaften zeigen, mich mit grossartigeren Bergen erfüllen und mein poetisches Können mehr stärken, als das Daheimbleiben hinter Büchern es gethan hätte" (KW. 3, 195 f.). Sie zeigt zugleich, wie Keats die Inspiration zu seinen Naturschilderungen am Herzen der Natur selbst suchte.

Was endlich Stoff und Handlung des *Hyperion* betrifft, so hat Keats hierfür eine bestimmte Quelle nicht gehabt. Er sammelte seine Kenntnis des Titanenkampfes aus Büchern wie Lemprieres *Classical Dictionary*, Spence's *Polymetis* und Tooke's *Pantheon*, sowie aus zerstreuten Angaben klassischer Schriftsteller, insbesondere Ovid und Hesiod, wobei er lateinische und griechische Ideen und Namen nicht selten kritiklos vermischte. Aber die ganze Anlage der Handlung, die Charaktere und Einzelheiten sind Schöpfungen seiner eignen Einbildungskraft.

IV. Die Ueberarbeitung des *Hyperion* als Vision.

Woodhouse bemerkt, in Uebereinstimmung mit dem zuletzt Gesagten, über den ursprünglichen Plan des *Hyperion*: „Das Gedicht würde, wenn es vollendet worden wäre, von der Entthronung des früheren Sonnengottes Hyperion durch Apollo — und beiläufig von derjenigen des Oceanus durch Neptun, des Saturn durch Jupiter etc. und von dem Kriege der Riesen behufs Wiedereinsetzung Saturns — gehandelt haben, nebst andern Ereignissen, von denen wir in den mythologischen Dichtern Griechenlands und Roms nur sehr dunkle Andeutungen haben. Die Ereignisse würden in

Wirklichkeit reine Schöpfungen der Phantasie des Dichters gewesen sein" (KW. 2. 144).

Weshalb hat Keats den *Hyperion* nicht vollendet? — Seinen eignen Aeusserungen zufolge war seine veränderte Stellung zu Milton von massgebender Bedeutung für das Fallenlassen des ursprünglichen Plans. In dem schon kurz berührten Brief an Reynolds vom 22. Sept. 1819 heisst es:

„Ich habe *Hyperion* aufgegeben — es waren zu viele Miltonische Inversionen darin. Miltonische Poesie kann nur in künstlerischer oder richtiger Künstlerstimmung geschrieben werden. Ich möchte mich andern Gefühlen hingeben. Das Englische sollte hochgehalten werden. Es dürfte dich interessieren, einige Verse vom *Hyperion* auszulesen und mit einem ✝ die falsche Schönheit zu bezeichnen, die aus der Kunst entspringt, und mit || die wahre Stimme des Gefühls. Bei meiner Seele, es war Phantasie — ich kann den Unterschied nicht machen — Hin und wieder ist Miltonische Stimmung darin — Aber ich kann die Abgrenzung nicht richtig machen" (Lett. ed. Forman 380).

In einem langen Schreiben an George aus denselben Tagen drückt er sich noch stärker aus:

„Ich werde mich nie für ein fremdes Idiom so erwärmen, dass ich es in meine Schriften einfliessen liesse. Das *Verlorne Paradies*, obwohl so schön an und für sich, ist eine Verfälschung unserer Sprache (a corruption of our language). Es sollte geachtet werden als das, was es ist, eigenartig, eine Seltenheit — eine schöne, grossartige Seltenheit, die merkwürdigste Schöpfung der Welt, worin ein nördlicher Dialekt sich griechischen und lateinischen Inversionen und Intonationen anpasst. Das reinste Englisch — oder was das reinste sein sollte - ist meiner Ansicht nach Chatterton's. . . . . Chatterton's Sprache ist vollständig nördlich. Ich ziehe die natürliche Musik derselben Miltons metrisch gemessener vor. Ich bin erst seit kurzem auf meiner Hut vor Milton. Leben für ihn würde Tod für mich sein. Miltonische Poesie kann nicht ge-

schrieben werden, sondern ist die Poesie der Kunst. Ich
wünsche mich ganz einer andern Poesie zu widmen" (KW.
4, 30 f. Lett. ed. Form. 418 f.).

Dieser Wandel in seiner Beurteilung Miltons muss sich
ziemlich plötzlich im Lauf des September 1819 vollzogen
haben. Hatte er doch noch Ende August desselben Jahres erklärt, Shakespeare und das *Verlorne Paradies* würden täglich
grössere Wunder für ihn (s. oben S. 18).

Unter „Miltonischen Inversionen" sind offenbar unenglische Konstruktionen zu verstehen, wie sie Milton unter
lateinischem und griechischem Einfluss zahlreich hat. Verunglückte Satzbildungen dieser Art finden sich im „Hyperion"
gelegentlich. W. T. Arnold[1] weist auf Stellen wie:

„Save what solemn tubes,
Blown by the serious Zephyrs, gave of sweet
And wandering sounds" (1, 206—8)

und:

„At whose joys . . . .
I, Coelus, wonder, how they came and whence;
And at the fruits thereof what shapes they be" (1, 312 -15)

hin, die er vergleicht mit PL. 2, 20 f.

„With what besides in council or in fight
Hath been achieved of merit".

bezw. PL. 2, 990

„I know thee, stranger, who thou art."

Aber besonders häufig sind solche Konstruktionen im *Hyperion* keineswegs. Sie kommen anderseits auch in der überarbeiteten Fassung desselben, sowie in andern Keats'schen
Gedichten vor; und der Dichter Robert Bridges[2] betont

---

[1] Einleitung seiner Ausg. S. XXXI.

[2] In seiner kritischen Einleitung zu Drury's Ausgabe der
Gedichte (London, Lawrence & Bullen, 1896) S. XLIII ff. Die
Einleitung ist auch separat gedruckt u. d. T.: *John Keats, A critical
Essay*. By Robert Bridges. Privately printed. 1895. (S. 35 ff.)

mit Recht, dass die richtig gehandhabte Inversion geradezu eins der allerwichtigsten und unentbehrlichsten poetischen Kunstmittel sei.

Es ist kaum glaublich, dass diese formalen Mängel allein die Schuld an dem Fallenlassen der ersten Fassung tragen. Der Aerger darüber mag dem Fass den Boden ausgeschlagen haben: so gut wie aufgegeben hatte Keats die Dichtung nach Woodhouse's Zeugnis schon im Frühjahr 1819, als sie den gegenwärtigen Umfang erreicht hatte. Damals aber stand er noch ganz im Banne Miltons.

Wir werden deshalb die Hauptmotive doch wohl anderswo zu suchen haben. Zunächst war der grosse Vorkämpfer des Puritanismus dem Dichter von *Isabella*, *Eve of St. Agnes*, *Eve of St. Mark* und *La Belle Dame sans Merci* offenbar zu wenig kongenial. Indem Keats im *Hyperion* seinen Spuren folgte, arbeitete er mit dem drückenden Gefühl bewusster Nachahmung; und obwohl er gerade jetzt das Höchste leistete, fühlte er sich doch aus seinen eignen Bahnen gerissen.

Dazu kommen Schwierigkeiten im Stoffe selbst. Wir haben schon darauf hingewiesen, dass im Verhältnis zu der grossartigen Anlage des Epos die über den Titanenkampf vorliegende klassische Ueberlieferung gar zu geringfügig war. Weitaus das Meiste, namentlich alle Einzelheiten, hätte von der Phantasie des Dichters frei ersonnen werden müssen, und das wäre bei diesem Thema selbst für ein Dichtergenie ersten Ranges vielleicht zu viel gewesen. Auch sonst bot der Stoff Klippen genug. Wie hätte Keats nach der unübertrefflichen Schilderung der cyklopischen Titanengestalten die siegreichen jüngeren Götter darstellen sollen? Sie müssen doch noch grösser und imponierender gezeichnet werden als jene. Dass ihm das gelungen wäre, ist nach dem ersten misslungenen Versuch im dritten Buch kaum wahrscheinlich. Wie kläglich führt sich Apollo ein! Ein hysterisches Weib, kein Gott! Es scheint wohl, als ob das Werk äusserlich zunächst an eben dieser Klippe gescheitert sei. —

Ueber *Hyperion, a Vision* schwebt ein neuer Stern: Dante. Keats kannte den Dichter der *Divina Commedia* in Cary's Uebersetzung schon seit 1817[1]). Im Studium desselben wurde er durch seinen Freund Bailey, einen Bewunderer des grossen Florentiners, nachdrücklichst bestärkt, und es ist bezeichnend genug, dass die einzigen Bücher, die der Dichter auf der schottischen Reise im Tornister bei sich trug, die drei kleinen Bändchen von Cary's Dante-Uebersetzung waren[2]).

Eine Frucht dieser Dante-Studien ist das Sonett *As Hermes once took to his feathers light*, welches Keats Anfang April 1819 in den ersten Band von Cary schrieb (KW. 2, 334 ff.). Es

---

[1]) *The Vision: or, Hell, Purgatory, and Paradise. of Dante Alighieri.* Translated by the Rev. H. F. Cary, A. M. In three volumes. London: Printed for Taylor and Hessey, 93, Fleet Street. 1814. — Taylor und Hessey haben auch *Endymion* und den *Lamia*-Band verlegt. Keats war im Frühjahr 1817 mit ihnen befreundet geworden. Es ist möglich, dass sie ihn auf Dante aufmerksam machten; möglich aber auch, dass es Bailey war, den er im Spätsommer 1817 zu Oxford kennen lernte. In einem Brief aus Oxford an seine Schwester Fanny vom 10. Sept. 1817 giebt er seiner Bewunderung für das Italienische Ausdruck: er meint, es sollte in allen Schulen des Landes an Stelle des Französischen treten. In dem Aufsatz über Kean, der am 21. Dez. 1817 erschien, findet sich schon ein Citat aus Cary's Dante. — Cary's Uebersetzung ist übrigens in der „Albion Edition" (Warne & Co.) heute allgemein zugänglich.

[2]) Vor dem Antritt der Reise, am 10. Juni 1818, schreibt er an Bailey: „Ich muss sagen, ich fühle jene Stelle aus Dante. Wenn ich irgend ein Buch mit mir nehme, sollen es jene winzigen Bände von Cary sein" (KW. 3, 160 f.) Und von Schottland aus schreibt er an denselben Freund: „Du sagst, ich müsse Dante studieren; nun, die einzigen Bücher, die ich mit mir habe, sind jene drei kleinen Bändchen" (KW. 3, 197).

ist der Ausfluss eines Traums, welcher durch die Lektüre der Episode von Paolo und Francesca veranlasst war[1]). Eine weitere Reminiszenz aus Dante sieht Hunt in der 2. Strophe des *Eve of St. Agnes*. (vgl. KW. 2, 72 f.; anm.). Ueberhaupt dürfte der mystische Hauch, der die „präraphaelitischen" Dichtungen *Eve of St. Agnes*, *Eve of St. Mark* und *La Belle Dame sans Merci* durchweht, zum Teil in Dante seine Quelle haben. Dagegen finden wir in der gleichzeitig mit jenen entstandenen ersten Fassung des *Hyperion* von einem Einfluss Dantes keine Spur. Die Schilderung der gestürzten Titanen in der Unterwelt hätte ja allenfalls Gelegenheit dazu geboten; aber die Höllenknechte des *Inferno* konnten als Vorbilder jener gigantischen Elementargottheiten unmöglich in Betracht kommen; Keats ist mit richtigem Instinkt hier Miltons Spuren gefolgt.

Im September 1819 begann der Dichter in Winchester mit grossem Eifer Italienisch zu lernen und brachte es in kurzer Zeit so weit, dass er Ariost und Dante in der Ursprache lesen konnte[2]). Durch dies Studium scheint seine Bewunderung für die *Divina Commedia* neue Nahrung erhalten zu haben. So wird es begreiflich, wenn dieselbe auf die Gestaltung der bald darauf begonnenen Ueberarbeitung des *Hyperion* einen so bedeutenden Einfluss gewann. Die Lektüre Dantes hat Keats auf den seltsamen Gedanken gebracht, *Hyperion* in die Form einer Vision umzugiessen, die Geschichte vom Sturz der Titanen als Offenbarung einer Göttin des gestürzten Geschlechts darzustellen. Vielleicht war der Titel *The Vision*, den Cary seiner Uebersetzung der *Divina Commedia* gab, nicht ohne Einfluss. Nachwirkungen der Lektüre des italienischen Originals, die Bridges (S. 140) in der Sprache der Keats'schen Vision entdeckt haben will, sind zu unkon-

---

[1]) Der Traum ist beschrieben in einem Brief an George v. 15. April 1819 (KW. 3. 284. Lett. ed. Form. 315).

[2]) KW. 2. 72 f., anm. 3, 327. 4. 30.

trollierbar. Dagegen zeigt der Eingang der beiden Dichtungen
eine unverkennbare Parallele. Wie die *Divina Commedia* in
einem Walde, so beginnt *Hyperion, a Vision* in einem Blüten-
garten. Wie Dante durch Virgil und Beatrice, so wird
Keats durch Moneta-Mnemosyne geführt.

Die Titanin Mnemosyne spielt im ersten Entwurf die
Rolle einer Vermittlerin zwischen den alten und jungen
Göttern. In der letzten Szene des Fragments teilt sie
Apollo von ihrer Weisheit mit, wodurch er sich erst seiner
göttlichen Natur und Sendung bewusst wird. An diese Gestalt knüpft der Dichter in der *Vision* an, aber sie erscheint
hier unter dem Namen Moneta: nur einmal (v. 307) wird
sie in der *Vision* Mnemosyne genannt, wofür aber gleich darauf
(v. 313) wieder Moneta eintritt. Keats hatte 1819 ein
lateinisches Buch über Mythologie gekauft: *Auctores Mytho-
graphi Latini*. Hier fand er S. 4 eine Bemerkung über die
Göttin Moneta, die ihn veranlasste, die griechische Mnemosyne, die Mutter der Musen, mit der römischen Moneta zu
identifizieren [1]).

Die Dichtung zerfällt von selbst in zwei Teile: nur der
erste, d. h. die Einleitung (bis 266) ist neu, der zweite
enthält die Bearbeitung des ursprünglichen Gedichts. Die
Kritiker stimmen wohl alle darin überein, dass die Einleitung
das Bedeutendste am ganzen Werke ist. Die ersten 18 Verse
allerdings sind herzlich schwach und geschmacklos; auch
sonst finden sich gelegentlich minderwertige Stellen. Im
allgemeinen aber zeigt sich hier die alte Kraft noch unge-
brochen, wenn auch falsch angewandt. Die hehre, über-
menschliche Gestalt der Saturnpriesterin reiht sich den
Titanen des ersten Entwurfs ebenbürtig an. Es ist unrichtig,
wenn der Diktion ein Zurückfallen in die Fehler der Endy-
mion-Periode vorgeworfen wird: die Sprache ist im Gegen-

---

[1]) Colvin, Keats S. 186.

teil vielfach klassisch schön und einfach: und die Schilderung der Vision ist entschieden in ihrer Art eine achtenswerte Leistung, wenn auch nicht gerade „generally worthy to be reckoned with Keats' best work", wie Bridges (S. 43) meint.

Das Neue, Eigenartige an der Dichtung liegt darin, dass sie eine beabsichtigte Allegorie ist. Sie ist, gleich der *Divina Commedia*, ein Ausfluss der bittern Lebenserfahrungen des Dichters; sie soll in allegorischer Form die Gefühle und Gedanken aussprechen, die ihn damals bedrückten. Dadurch gewinnt sie ein eignes, persönliches Interesse, wie es in dieser Weise keins der übrigen Gedichte hat. Nirgends entwickelt Keats seine Auffassung des Dichterberufs, seine Erfahrungen vom Dichterlose so eingehend wie hier. Die *Vision* knüpft an *Sleep and Poetry* an, aber der Fortschritt der Weltanschauung seit jenem Jugendgedicht ist ein bedeutender.

Die Grundgedanken der Allegorie sind im allgemeinen klar, wenn auch über die Deutung der Einzelheiten Zweifel herrschen können. Die folgende Auslegung weicht von den Erklärungsversuchen Colvin's und namentlich Bridges'[1]) in manchen wesentlichen Punkten ab. Der Visionär ist der Dichter selbst, ist der Träumer, der ein Ideal verfolgt, seinen Träumen nachhängt und darüber die praktische Lebensführung gern vernachlässigt. Der paradiesische Garten, in dem er sich ergeht, ist das Reich der Schönheit, der berauschende Trank aus den Früchten dieses Gartens die Poesie, die dem Dichter alle Sinne berückt und Willen und Verstand in Fesseln schlägt. Das Heiligtum des Saturn, in dem er sich bei seinem Erwachen findet, ist das Reich der Ewigkeit, die Stufen, die zum Altar führen (these immortal steps 1, 117) sind die Stufen zur

---

[1]) Colvin, Keats S. 188 f. Bridges, John Keats S. 43 ff.

menschlichen Unsterblichkeit[1]). Darüber ragt riesenhoch in den Wolken verschwindend das Bild der Unendlichkeit, der Ewigkeit empor. Mnemosyne, die Mutter der Musen, der Kunst, des Gesanges, ist die Priesterin dieses Tempels der Unsterblichkeit. Der Zutritt zu dem Heiligtum wird nur den Träumern verstattet, gewissermassen als Entgelt für das Uebermass von Leid und Qualen, die sie auf Erden ertragen. Die gewöhnlichen Sterblichen, auch die Besten unter ihnen, deren ganzes Denken und Trachten auf die Welt der Wirklichkeit, auf das Wohl ihrer Mitmenschen gerichtet ist, kommen nicht hierher und tragen auch kein Verlangen danach. Sie sind besser als die schwächlichen Träumer, die der Welt nichts nützen, sie finden deshalb ihr Glück und ihren Lohn im Leben selbst. Von den Dichtern und Träumern aber, die in den Tempel der Ewigkeit zugelassen werden, gelangen nur diejenigen zu den höchsten Stufen der Unsterblichkeit, die sich ein lebendiges Gefühl für „den Riesenschmerz der Welt" (the giant agony of the world 1, 157) bewahren, die, um mit Faust zu reden, es über sich gewinnen, neben der Menschheit Wohl auch der Menschheit Weh auf ihren Busen zu häufen.

"None can usurp this height", return'd that shade,
"But those to whom the miseries of the world
Are misery, and will not let them rest.

---

[1]) Robert Bridges (S. 44) meint: „His awaking in the temple is his recovery from this (d. i. state of selfish isolation) to a sympathy with the miseries of the world: and the temple itself is the temple of knowledge, which it is death for a visionary to enter if he have not that sympathy. The steps to the altar are the struggle of such a mind to reach truth: and truth itself is revealed by knowledge." Der Saturntempel ein Tempel der Erkenntnis ist jedenfalls höchst unwahrscheinlich. Auch die übrigen Erklärungen entsprechen dem Wortlaut und Gedankengang der Dichtung nicht.

All else who find a haven in the world.
Where they may thoughtless sleep away their days,
If by a chance into this fane they come,
Rot on the pavement where thou rottedst half" (1. 147—153).

Alle diejenigen, die sich in selbstsüchtigem Quietismus auf sich selbst zurückziehen, sich dem Elend der Welt verschliessen, die werden, sofern ihnen überhaupt der Anblick der Unsterblichkeit vergönnt wird, auf dem grabeskalten Niveau der Gewöhnlichkeit ihre Tage beschliessen und rasch vergessen sein.

Diese Auffassung von den Aufgaben des Menschen auf Erden und insbesondere von den Pflichten und der Verantwortung des Dichterberufs, die an Schiller erinnert, ist bei Keats nicht neu. Auch früher hatte er das Leben der That über das der Gedanken und Träume gestellt, aber nirgends so eindringlich und überzeugungsvoll wie hier. Sein eignes bisheriges Dichterleben erscheint ihm jetzt selbstsüchtig: nur mit Mühe vermag er die erste Stufe zur Unsterblichkeit zu erklimmen. Und doch hatte er in Wahrheit gerade in dieser Periode, wo er ganz der Poesie lebte, der Menschheit am meisten genützt! Diese seltsame Verkennung und Missachtung des Wertes dichterischer Produktion, diese Bitterkeit, mit der er von dem traurigen Los des Dichters überhaupt spricht („Only the dreamer venoms all his days. Bearing more woe than all his sins deserve" 1, 175 f.), lässt uns einen tiefen Blick in das geistige und körperliche Elend thun, aus dem diese Dichtung hervorquoll, lässt uns ahnen, wie tief Keats, der noch vor wenigen Jahren mit schwellender Hoffnung sich ganz der Poesie verschrieb, den Kainsfluch des Genies an sich selbst erfahren hatte.

So interessant, ja bedeutend dieser originelle, erste Teil der Dichtung für sich genommen ist, so verfehlt ist er jedenfalls als Einleitung zu einem Hyperion-Epos. Der

Stoff des letzteren ist ja freilich erhaben genug: eine neue *Göttliche Komödie* aber liess sich unmöglich daraus schaffen. Der Versuch, den Sturz des Titanengeschlechts in die Form einer Offenbarung der Titanin Moneta-Mnemosyne an den verzückten Dichter zu schildern und zu diesem Zweck die erste Fassung des *Hyperion* mit jener Vision zu verweben, konnte nur zu einer Verstümmelung der grossartigen Gemälde des ersten Entwurfes führen. Bridges freilich (S. 42) schliesst aus der Verschmelzung der beiden, dass auch der alte *Hyperion* eine tiefere allegorische Bedeutung hatte; doch dürfte er mit dieser Auffassung schwerlich Beifall finden. Dem ersten Entwurf lag allerdings die Idee zu Grunde, dass eine ältere, rohere Generation mit Naturnotwendigkeit einer jüngeren, ihr geistig überlegenen den Platz räumen muss. Aber von einer derartigen Grundidee bis zur Allegorie ist doch noch ein weiter Schritt.

Der zweite Teil der *Vision* ist ein trauriges Beispiel dafür, wie ein bedeutender Dichter im Stadium des Verfalls seiner poetischen Kraft eins seiner schönsten Werke mit eigner Hand zerstören kann. Die vermeintlichen Besserungen sind wohl ausnahmslos Verschlechterungen. Die meisten derselben wurden durch die Umwandlung des Epos in die Form der Vision veranlasst: was früher objektive Erzählung war, wird jetzt zum Bericht des Visionärs als Augenzeugen; zudem wird der Fortgang der Schilderung wiederholt durch Erklärungen der Führerin unterbrochen. Andere Aenderungen beruhen auf dem Streben, die „Miltonschen Inversionen" des ersten Entwurfs zu beseitigen: die oben (S. 29) citierte Stelle 1, 206—8 z. B. ist in der zweiten Fassung (2, 50) weggelassen. Ferner ist das Landschaftsbild am Eingang in der *Vision* düsterer gemalt als im alten *Hyperion*: statt „No stir of air was there" (1, 7) heisst es in der jüngeren Version: „No stir of life was in this *shrouded* vale" (1, 286 f.); statt „By reason of his fallen divinity

Spreading a shade" (1. 12 f.) heisst es dort: „By reason of the fallen divinity Spreading *more* shade" (1. 292 f.). sicherlich keine Verbesserung. Verschiedene schöne Stellen sind ohne besondern Grund den vermeintlichen Besserungsversuchen zum Opfer gefallen (vgl. Hyp. 1. 73 f. mit Vision 1. 349 und Hyp. 1. 86 mit Vis. 1. 359), während anderseits wirklich geschmacklose Wendungen wie 1, 8 f. unverändert beibehalten sind (1. 287 ff.). Auf eine interessante Ursache von Veränderungen macht Bridges (S. 39) aufmerksam. Eine alte Gewohnheit von Keats war die übermässige Verwendung der Vokativ-Partikel O!, die namentlich im *Endymion* sehr häufig ist. Die wenigen Stellen, wo sie im *Hyperion* I sich findet, sind in der *Vision* grundsätzlich geändert, so dass in letzterer kein einziges O! beibehalten ist. Daraus ergab sich dann leicht die Notwendigkeit weiterer Aenderungen. Man vergleiche nur Hyp. 1, 50—56 mit Vision 1. 328—34 und besonders Hyp. 1. 68 mit Vis. 1. 344, wo für O thoughtless sogar der Latinismus me thoughtless eingeführt ist.

Keats hat nur einige Stücke aus dem ersten Buch bearbeitet; dann gab er auch die zweite Fassung auf und bald genug das Dichten überhaupt. Die verhängnisvolle Krankheit setzte aller weiteren Thätigkeit ein jähes Ende.

V. Bibliographisches.

1. *Hyperion.*

Ein Originalmanuskript des *Hyperion* ist uns nicht erhalten. Die Textgrundlage für kritische Ausgaben ist der einzige vom Dichter selbst besorgte Druck in dem Band von 1820, wo unser Fragment den Schluss bildet (S. 143—199). Einen genauen Abdruck dieses Bandes nebst eingehender Beschreibung giebt Forman in seiner gleich zu nennenden Gesamtausgabe (II. 1 ff.). Der Band ist in 12°, der Druck mässig gross, die Zeilen ziemlich weit auseinander, 18 auf der Seite. Die Verse sind nicht numeriert.

Ausser diesem autorisierten Druck ist eine **frühere Fassung in einer von Woodhouse veranlassten Abschrift** aus dem Sommer 1819 erhalten. Diese Abschrift findet sich in einem „Commonplace book" Woodhouses, einem über 300 Seiten dicken Lederband in Quart, der aus Woodhouses Händen in den Besitz des Verlegers Taylor überging und jetzt Sidney Colvin gehört (vgl. die Vorrede zu dessen Keats-Biographie S. VII f.). Für die liebenswürdige Ueberlassung desselben bin ich Prof. Colvin zu grossem Dank verpflichtet.

Der Band enthält Abschriften von vielen damals unveröffentlichten Werken des Dichters. Sie sind grösstenteils in Woodhouses eigner kursiven, recht gefälligen Hand; aber gerade *Hyperion* macht eine Ausnahme: er ist unter Woodhouses Aufsicht von einem Schreiber kopiert. Dieser liess vielfach bei Eigennamen und andern selteneren Wörtern, die ihm nicht geläufig waren, Lücken offen, welche dann von Woodhouse selbst ausgefüllt wurden. Auch Schreibfehler des Kopisten sind öfters von ihm verbessert. Alle seine Nachträge sind mit Tinte gemacht; seine Hand ist unverkennbar, auch die Tinte von der des Schreibers verschieden[1]).

Der *Hyperion* umfasst die Seiten 39—99 des Commonplace book; doch sind immer nur die Vorderseiten beschrieben. Die Blätter sind ziemlich eng liniert; rechts

---

[1]) In den Versen 806—29 auf S. 93 (d. i. 3, 53—76) nimmt die Handschrift der Kopie plötzlich einen ganz veränderten Charakter an; sie ist steiler und runder als überall sonst; aber die Tinte ist die gleiche, und es ist kaum wahrscheinlich, dass es die Hand eines andern Schreibers ist.

und links laufen Randlinien herunter. Am Rande und auf den leeren Rückseiten finden sich Bleistiftnotizen und -Zeichen, und im Texte selbst ist die ursprüngliche Lesart verschiedentlich in die gedruckte korrigiert. Die allermeisten dieser Noten und Korrekturen rühren augenscheinlich von späteren Händen, von Mitgliedern der Familie Taylor her und haben für die Geschichte des Textes keinen Wert. Nur an ganz wenigen Stellen glaube ich des Dichters eigne Hand zu erkennen, die bei andern Gedichten in diesem Bande ziemlich häufig wiederkehrt. Auf Keats selbst geht wahrscheinlich die Streichung der Verse zurück, die ursprünglich hinter 1, 21 (Thus the old Eagle etc.), 1, 102 (What dost think? etc.) und vielleicht auch 3, 125 (Into a hue etc.) folgten. Diese Streichungen sind mit weichem Blei sehr sorgfältig ausgeführt, die beiden ersten von Woodhouse mit Tinte nachgezogen. Von Keats' Hand rührt meiner Ansicht nach ferner das Wherefore gegenüber 1, 190, die beiden qy zu 1, 277—80 und 1, 319 f., sowie der Versuch einer Vollendung des Schlussverses her. Auch diese Notizen sind in Blei. Woodhouse hat, von den Korrekturen der Kopie abgesehen, anscheinend nach der Drucklegung der Dichtung an der ursprünglichen Fassung nichts geändert. Wenn sich gleichwohl an zwei Stellen (1, 189 Savour of poisonous brass und 1, 200 When earthquakes jar their battlements and towers) die gedruckte Lesart mit Tinte von seiner Hand eingetragen findet, so geschah dies wohl vor der Drucklegung auf Anweisung des Dichters selbst. Möglicher Weise sind alle diese genannten Besserungen aus Besprechungen des Dichters mit Woodhouse hervorgegangen.

Die Einteilung nach Büchern deckt sich in der älteren Fassung genau mit derjenigen der gedruckten Ausgabe von 1820. Aber während letztere keine Verszählung hat, sind in Woodhouses Abschrift die Verse von 10 zu 10 numeriert, und zwar nicht innerhalb der Bücher, sondern von Anfang bis Ende durch: im ganzen 891 und ein Wort. Doch hatte der Schreiber den Vers „Look up, and let me see our doom in it" (1. 97) infolge gleichen Anfangs mit dem folgenden zuerst ausgelassen und erst nachträglich eingefügt, dann aber nicht weiter mitgezählt, sodass Woodhouses Version thatsächlich 892 Verse und ein Wort umfasst. Davon sind in dem gedruckten Text 9 Verse gestrichen, sodass also für diesen 883 und ein Wort übrig bleiben (vgl. oben S. 8).

Die beiden Fassungen stimmen in ihrem Wortlaut im grossen und ganzen genau überein: indessen finden sich ausser den 9 später gestrichenen Versen in der älteren Version doch manche kleinere Abweichungen. Es ist nicht uninteressant, die gedruckte Fassung einerseits mit diesen und anderseits mit der späteren Ueberarbeitung des Textes in der *Vision* zu vergleichen. Während letztere von jedem als eine Verstümmelung des ursprünglichen Gedichts empfunden wird, kennzeichnen sich die Aenderungen des gedruckten Textes gegenüber der älteren, Woodhouseschen Version durchweg als entschiedene Verbesserungen.

Die beste neuere Ausgabe des *Hyperion* ist die von Buxton Forman in seiner grossen Gesamtausgabe: *The Poetical Works and other Writings of John Keats*. Edited, with notes and appendices, by H. Buxton Forman. In four volumes. London, Reeves & Turner. 1883. 8°. Reissue, with additions and corrections, 1889. Dies Werk, das sich durch eine bewunderungswürdige Vollständigkeit auszeichnet und mit kritischen Beigaben versehen ist, bildet die unentbehrliche Grundlage für jeden Keatsforscher[1]). Der Text des *Hyperion* ist ein genauer Nachdruck aus dem Band von 1820. Nur in 7 Fällen hat Forman die Schreibung normalisiert: sie sind in der Vorrede zu Bd. I, S. XLV und XLVII gewissenhaft verzeichnet. An allen diesen Stellen

---

[1]) In der vorliegenden Ausgabe citiert als KW.

stimmt die Schreibung des Woodhouse-Textes mit der gedruckten Ausgabe überein; nur 3, 114 hat jener grey wie Forman, nicht gray.

Einen zuverlässigen Textabdruck aus der grossen, aber ohne den kritischen Apparat derselben, giebt Forman in seiner kleineren Ausgabe: *The Poetical Works of John Keats. Given from his own editions and other authentic sources, and collated with many manuscripts. Edited by H. Buxton Forman. London, Reeves & Turner, 1884. 8°. 6. Aufl. 1898. Pr. 8 s.* Diese vortrefflich ausgestattete, mit 7 Porträts und 10 andern Abbildungen versehene Ausgabe ist für den gewöhnlichen Bedarf am meisten zu empfehlen. Die oben erwähnten graphischen Abweichungen vom Originaldruck finden sich auch hier.

Von den zahlreichen übrigen Ausgaben der poetischen Werke sei wegen ihrer trefflichen Einleitung über Keats' poetischen Stil und dessen Quellen hervorgehoben die von W. T. Arnold: *The Poetical Works of John Keats*. London: Kegan Paul, Trench & Co. 1884. Später datiert 1888. Pr. 3 s. 6 d.

W. T. Arnold hat auch die einzige nennenswerte Sonderausgabe des *Hyperion* für englische Schulen veranstaltet: doch umfasst sie nur das erste Buch: *Keats' Hyperion. Book I. Edited with notes by W. T. Arnold. Oxford, Clarendon Press, 1892. Pr. 4 d.* Die Anmerkungen sind zum Teil sehr lesenswert. Auf einen kritischen Text hat Arnold in beiden Ausgaben kein Gewicht gelegt.

Die Keats-Bibliographie bis 1886 findet man im Anhang zu W. M. Rossetti's *Life of J. K.* in den *Great Writers* annähernd vollständig zusammengestellt.

2. Vision.

Das Manuskript dieser Dichtung, das Monckton Milnes (der spätere Lord Houghton) von Keats' Freund Brown erhielt, wurde ihm später gestohlen[1]) und ist nicht wieder zum Vorschein gekommen.

In seinem *Life and Letters of J. K.* (1848) bezeichnet Milnes die *Vision* auf Grund der Angaben Browns richtig als eine Ueberarbeitung. Als er sie acht Jahre später im 3. Band der *Miscellanies of the Philobiblon Society* (1856—57) zum ersten Mal herausgab, hatte er das ausdrückliche Zeugnis Browns offenbar vergessen: denn er zweifelt jetzt, ob es eine ältere Fassung oder eine Umarbeitung sei und giebt ihr deshalb die Ueberschrift *Another Version of Keats's 'Hyperion'*. Beim Wiederabdruck im Anhang zur zweiten Auflage des *Life and Letters* 1867 erklärte Lord Houghton das Gedicht nunmehr zweifellos für den ersten Entwurf des *Hyperion*. Unter diesem Titel wurde es dann in alle Ausgaben der gesammelten Dichtungen aufgenommen, bis Sidney Colvin in seiner mustergültigen Keats-Biographie 1889 (S. 230—32) unwiderleglich nachwies, dass die *Vision* der Anfang einer **Ueberarbeitung** und keine ältere Fassung ist.

3. Die vorliegende Ausgabe.

Der Text der vorliegenden Ausgabe des *Hyperion* beruht auf dem Originaldruck von 1820. Titelblatt und Ueberschriften der drei Bücher sind möglichst ähnlich nachgebildet. Am Kopf der Seiten ist wie im Originaldruck ausser dem Kopftitel Hyperion auf der Innenseite in etwas kleineren Kapitalen auch das Buch angegeben. Im übrigen ist die Ausgabe natürlich keine facsimilierte Nachbildung, sondern nur ein genauer Abdruck des Originaltextes.

In der Normalisierung der Schreibung bin ich Forman nicht gefolgt, sondern habe mich auch in der Orthographie

---

[1]) Nach einer Mitteilung Formans, dem es der verstorbene Lord Houghton selbst sagte.

streng an den Originaldruck gehalten. Im übrigen unterscheidet sich der vorliegende Text von dem Forman's nur durch Hinzufügung der Varianten der Woodhouse-Version, welche Forman erst in einem Nachtrag zu seinem Werk verwerten konnte[1]). Sie sind zuerst von Colvin im Anhang seiner Keats-Biographie (S. 231 f.) abgedruckt worden. Die dort aufgeführten Lesarten liessen sich nur in Kleinigkeiten vervollständigen (vgl. besonders 1. 9). Die zahlreichen Abweichungen in Orthographie und Interpunktion habe ich natürlich nicht verzeichnet. Auch Schreibfehler und sonstige kleinere Verschiedenheiten sind unberücksichtigt geblieben[2]). Im übrigen darf man, wo keine Varianten vermerkt sind, annehmen, dass die beiden Fassungen sich decken.

Bei der *Vision* macht die Herstellung eines kritischen Textes einige Schwierigkeit. Da wir kein Manuskript besitzen, müssen die Abdrücke Lord Houghtons von 1856 und 1867 als Grundlage dienen. Diese aber stimmen unter sich in mehreren Punkten nicht überein. Wenn die zweite Auflage 2, 10 self-hid statt des reef-hid der ersten, wenn sie 2, 34 metals sick statt metal rich und 2, 60 roar statt river liest, so haben wir es hier augenscheinlich mit Druckfehlern zu thun, die aus der schlechten Handschrift Lord Houghtons entsprangen. Dass der Herausgeber freilich diese krassen Druckfehler übersah, ist nicht gerade vertrauenerweckend für die Zuverlässigkeit seines ersten Textes. Ein peinlich genauer Herausgeber vom Schlage Formans war Seine Lordship überhaupt nicht. Bei den meisten

---

[1]) KW. 2. Aufl. I. S. XLVII* ff.
[2]) So hat der Woodhouse-Text z. B. 1. 217 dove wing (mit ausradiertem s) für dove-wings; 2, 43 sunk für sank; 2, 108 mightiness; 2, 139 in the sign; 2, 167 o' für of; 2, 210 in action, free companionship; 2, 312 was f. were; 2, 359 said f. sad; 3, 27 Hyle's f. hazels; 3, 81 This f. Thus.

Abweichungen des Drucks von 1867 ist es deshalb schwer zu sagen, ob sie Korrekturen nach dem Originalmannskript oder willkürliche Aenderungen Lord Houghtons sind. So herrscht in der Wiedergabe der Endung -ed eine merkwürdige Inkonsequenz. In einer Reihe von Fällen hat der zweite Text -ed statt des -'d im ersten: 83 embossed, 116 gummed, 147 returned, 307 und 308 grieved, 317 venomed, 421 scrutinized, 2, 52 square-edged. Diesen stehen aber zwei andere Beispiele gegenüber, wo die zweite Version umgekehrt das -ed der ersten in -'d korrigiert: 87 look'd, 301 bow'd. Weitere Unterschiede sind: 145 Prophetess in der zweiten gegenüber prophetess der ersten; 345 slumbrous st. slumber's; 2, 54 eyes st. eye; 2, 18 dire st. drear; endlich die auffallendste von allen: 97 When statt des As der ersten!

Wenn nun Forman's Text der *Vision* wieder von beiden Versionen Houghtons in zahleichen kleineren Punkten abweicht, so erklärt sich dies durch die Normalisierung der Schreibung, die Forman nach seinen Bd. I, S. XL ff. entwickelten Grundsätzen natürlich auch in der *Vision* durchgeführt hat. Die meisten seiner Aenderungen betreffen die Endung -ed, wo er für die stummen -ed Houghtons meist -'d einsetzt: 5 Trac'd, 16 purpos'd, 78 confus'd, 93 soberpac'd, 107 pronounc'd, 132 ic'd, 137 Cry'd (st. Cried), 138 sav'd, 155 Encourag'd, 198 spar'd, 216 cry'd (st. cried), 233 pin'd, 243 Half-clos'd, 249 twing'd, 252 ask'd, 253 environ'd, 289 feather'd, 340 unpractis'd, 375 curs'd, 376 rais'd, 402 chang'd, 436 cry'd (st. cried); II: 26 bastion'd, 27 touch'd, 32 breath'd, 43 Amaz'd, 46 rous'd, 51 Reliev'd, 61 scar'd. Weitere Aenderungen Forman's sind: 67 grey st. gray, 97 mid-day st. midday, 238 lilly st. lily, 379 Goddess st. goddes; II: 1 may'st st. mayst, 4 might'st st. mightst. Ferner Abweichungen in der Interpunktion: 96 hat Houghton hinter flame einen Punkt, Forman gar kein Zeichen;

191 hat H. hinter feminine ein Komma, F. keins; 319 hat H. hinter up einen Punkt, F. ein Komma; 342 hat H. kein Anführungszeichen vor With, 356 kein Komma hinter curls, während F. solche setzt.

Ich habe es auch hier vorgezogen, bei der Herstellung des Textes möglichst konservativ zu verfahren, und bin deshalb, trotz der möglichen Ungenauigkeit desselben, grundsätzlich Houghton's verbessertem zweiten Abdruck gefolgt. In den wenigen Fällen, wo ich von diesem Prinzip abweiche (1, 416; 2. 57. 58), findet sich in den Fussnoten ein entsprechender Vermerk.

London, Sept. 1898.

Johannes Hoops.

HYPERION.

A FRAGMENT.

HYPERION.

BOOK I.

Deep in the shady sadness of a vale
Far sunken from the healthy breath of morn,
Far from the fiery noon, and eve's one star,
Sat gray-hair'd Saturn, quiet as a stone,
Still as the silence round about his lair;   5
Forest on forest hung about his head
Like cloud on cloud. No stir of air was there,
Not so much life as on a summer's day
Robs not one light seed from the feather'd grass,
But where the dead leaf fell, there did it rest.   10
A stream went voiceless by, still deadened more

W. = *Woodhouse-Version:* s. *Einleitung S. 39. Der Titel lautet auch bei* W. Hyperion.   5 ff. *Die Verszählung fehlt im Originaldruck.*   9 Robs not at all the dandelion's fleece; W.   11 *Bei* W. *ist* voiceless *aus* noiseless *korrigiert. Letzteres Vis. 291 wieder eingesetzt.*

By reason of his fallen divinity
Spreading a shade: the Naiad 'mid her reeds
Press'd her cold finger closer to her lips.

    Along the margin-sand large foot-marks went.   15
No further than to where his feet had stray'd,
And slept there since. Upon the sodden ground
His old right hand lay nerveless, listless, dead,
Unsceptred; and his realmless eyes were closed;
While his bow'd head seem'd list'ning to the Earth,   20
His ancient mother, for some comfort yet.

    It seem'd no force could wake him from his place;
But there came one, who with a kindred hand
Touch'd his wide shoulders, after bending low
With reverence, though to one who knew it not.   25
She was a Goddess of the infant world;
By her in stature the tall Amazon
Had stood a pigmy's height: she would have ta'en
Achilles by the hair and bent his neck;
Or with a finger stay'd Ixion's wheel.   30
Her face was large as that of Memphian sphinx,
Pedestal'd haply in a palace court,
When sages look'd to Egypt for their lore.
But oh! how unlike marble was that face:

---

    16 stay'd *W*. *Hinter 21 folgt in W. ein Absatz von vier Versen, der anscheinend vom Dichter eigenhändig ausgestrichen ist:*
        Thus the old Eagle drowsy with great grief
          Sat moulting his weak plumage, never more
          To be restored or soar against the Sun;
          While his three Sons upon Olympus stood.
30 eased Ixion's toil *W*.

How beautiful, if sorrow had not made 35
Sorrow more beautiful than Beauty's self.
There was a listening fear in her regard,
As if calamity had but begun;
As if the vanward clouds of evil days
Had spent their malice, and the sullen rear 40
Was with its stored thunder labouring up.
One hand she press'd upon that aching spot
Where beats the human heart, as if just there,
Though an immortal, she felt cruel pain:
The other upon Saturn's bended neck 45
She laid, and to the level of his ear
Leaning with parted lips, some words she spake
In solemn tenour and deep organ tone:
Some mourning words, which in our feeble tongue
Would come in these like accents; O how frail 50
To that large utterance of the early Gods!
"Saturn, look up! — though wherefore, poor old King?
"I have no comfort for thee, no not one:
"I cannot say, 'O wherefore sleepest thou?'
"For heaven is parted from thee, and the earth 55
"Knows thee not, thus afflicted, for a God;
"And ocean too, with all its solemn noise,
"Has from thy sceptre pass'd; and all the air
"Is emptied of thine hoary majesty.
"Thy thunder, conscious of the new command, 60
"Rumbles reluctant o'er our fallen house;
"And thy sharp lightning in unpractised hands
"Scorches and burns our once serene domain.

"O aching time! O moments big as years!
"All as ye pass swell out the monstrous truth,   65
"And press it so upon our weary griefs
"That unbelief has not a space to breathe.
"Saturn, sleep on: — O thoughtless, why did I
"Thus violate thy slumbrous solitude?
"Why should I ope thy melancholy eyes?   70
"Saturn, sleep on! while at thy feet I weep."

 As when, upon a tranced summer-night,
Those green-rob'd senators of mighty woods,
Tall oaks, branch-charmed by the earnest stars,
Dream, and so dream all night without a stir,   75
Save from one gradual solitary gust
Which comes upon the silence, and dies off,
As if the ebbing air had but one wave;
So came these words and went; the while in tears
She touch'd her fair large forehead to the ground,   80
Just where her falling hair might be outspread
A soft and silken mat for Saturn's feet.
One moon, with alteration slow, had shed
Her silver seasons four upon the night,
And still these two were postured motionless,   85
Like natural sculpture in cathedral cavern;
The frozen God still couchant on the earth,
And the sad Goddess weeping at his feet:
Until at length old Saturn lifted up
His faded eyes, and saw his kingdom gone,   90
And all the gloom and sorrow of the place,
And that fair kneeling Goddess; and then spake,

---

 65 Each *st.* All *W.* 76 sudden *st.* gradual *W.*

As with a palsied tongue, and while his beard
Shook horrid with such aspen-malady:
"O tender spouse of gold Hyperion,   95
"Thea, I feel thee ere I see thy face;
"Look up, and let me see our doom in it;
"Look up, and tell me if this feeble shape
"Is Saturn's; tell me, if thou hear'st the voice
"Of Saturn; tell me, if this wrinkling brow,   100
"Naked and bare of its great diadem,
"Peers like the front of Saturn. Who had power
"To make me desolate? whence came the strength?
"How was it nurtur'd to such bursting forth,
"While Fate seem'd strangled in my nervous grasp? 105
"But it is so; and I am smother'd up,
"And buried from all godlike exercise
"Of influence benign on planets pale,
"Of admonitions to the winds and seas,
"Of peaceful sway above man's harvesting,   110
"And all those acts which Deity supreme
"Doth ease its heart of love in. — I am gone
"Away from my own bosom: I have left
"My strong identity, my real self,
"Somewhere between the throne, and where I sit   115
"Here on this spot of earth. Search, Thea, search!
"Open thine eyes eterne, and sphere them round
"Upon all space: space starr'd, and lorn of light;
"Space region'd with life-air; and barren void;

---

102 *Zwischen* Saturn *u.* Who *hat W.*: What dost think? Am I that same? — O Chaos! *Mit Blei und Tinte gestrichen; die Bleistriche älter als die Tintenstriche; erstere wohl von Keats selbst, letztere von Woodhouse. S. Einl. S. 40.* 116 bit *st.* spot *W.*

"Spaces of fire, and all the yawn of hell. — 120
"Search, Thea, search! and tell me, if thou seest
"A certain shape or shadow, making way
"With wings or chariot fierce to repossess
"A heaven he lost erewhile: it must — it must
"Be of ripe progress — Saturn must be King. 125
"Yes, there must be a golden victory;
"There must be Gods thrown down, and trumpets blown
"Of triumph calm, and hymns of festival
"Upon the gold clouds metropolitan,
"Voices of soft proclaim, and silver stir 130
"Of strings in hollow shells; and there shall be
"Beautiful things made new, for the surprise
"Of the sky-children; I will give command:
"Thea! Thea! Thea! where is Saturn?"

 This passion lifted him upon his feet, 135
And made his hands to struggle in the air,
His Druid locks to shake and ooze with sweat,
His eyes to fever out, his voice to cease.
He stood, and heard not Thea's sobbing deep;
A little time, and then again he snatch'd 140
Utterance thus. — "But cannot I create?
"Cannot I form? Cannot I fashion forth
"Another world, another universe,
"To overbear and crumble this to nought?
"Where is another chaos? Where?" — That word 145
Found way unto Olympus, and made quake
The rebel three. — Thea was startled up,
And in her bearing was a sort of hope,
As thus she quick-voic'd spake, yet full of awe.

"This cheers our fallen house: come to our friends, 150
"O Saturn! come away, and give them heart:
"I know the covert, for thence came I hither."
Thus brief; then with beseeching eyes she went
With backward footing through the shade a space:
He follow'd, and she turn'd to lead the way 155
Through aged boughs, that yielded like the mist
Which eagles cleave upmounting from their nest.

Meanwhile in other realms big tears were shed.
More sorrow like to this, and such like woe,
Too huge for mortal tongue or pen of scribe: 160
The Titans fierce, self-hid, or prison-bound,
Groan'd for the old allegiance once more,
And listen'd in sharp pain for Saturn's voice.
But one of the whole mammoth-brood still kept
His sov'reignty, and rule, and majesty: — 165
Blazing Hyperion on his orbed fire
Still sat, still snuff'd the incense, teeming up
From man to the sun's God: yet unsecure:
For as among us mortals omens drear
Fright and perplex, so also shuddered he — 170
Not at dog's howl, or gloom-bird's hated screech,
Or the familiar visiting of one
Upon the first toll of his passing-bell,
Or prophesyings of the midnight lamp;
But horrors, portion'd to a giant nerve, 175
Oft made Hyperion ache. His palace bright
Bastion'd with pyramids of glowing gold,

---

156 that gave to them like Mist *W*.

And touch'd with shade of bronzed obelisks,
Glar'd a blood-red through all its thousand courts,
Arches, and domes, and fiery galleries; 180
And all its curtains of Aurorian clouds
Flush'd angerly: while sometimes eagle's wings,
Unseen before by Gods or wondering men,
Darken'd the place; and neighing steeds were heard,
Not heard before by Gods or wondering men. 185
Also, when he would taste the spicy wreaths
Of incense, breath'd aloft from sacred hills,
Instead of sweets, his ample palate took
Savour of poisonous brass and metal sick:
And so, when harbour'd in the sleepy west, 190
After the full completion of fair day, —
For rest divine upon exalted couch
And slumber in the arms of melody,
He pac'd away the pleasant hours of ease
With stride colossal, on from hall to hall; 195
While far within each aisle and deep recess,
His winged minions in close clusters stood,
Amaz'd and full of fear; like anxious men
Who on wide plains gather in panting troops,
When earthquakes jar their battlements and towers. 200
Even now, while Saturn, rous'd from icy trance,
Went step for step with Thea through the woods.

---

189 A poison-feel of brass *W. Echt Keatsisch! Vergl. Einleitung S. 40.* 190 *Zu* And so *bei W. in Bleistift* Wherefore, *wohl von des Dichters Hand.* 199 on wide plain *W.: vgl. Vis. 2, 44* Who on a wide plain gather in sad troops. 200 When an Earthquake hath shook their City towers *W.*

Hyperion, leaving twilight in the rear,
Came slope upon the threshold of the west:
Then, as was wont, his palace-door flew ope   205
In smoothest silence, save what solemn tubes,
Blown by the serious Zephyrs, gave of sweet
And wandering sounds, slow-breathed melodies;
And like a rose in vermeil tint and shape,
In fragrance soft, and coolness to the eye,   210
That inlet to severe magnificence
Stood full blown, for the God to enter in.

He enter'd, but he enter'd full of wrath;
His flaming robes stream'd out beyond his heels,
And gave a roar, as if of earthly fire,   215
That scar'd away the meek ethereal Hours
And made their dove-wings tremble. On he flared,
From stately nave to nave, from vault to vault,
Through bowers of fragrant and enwreathed light,
And diamond-paved lustrous long arcades,   220
Until he reach'd the great main cupola;
There standing fierce beneath, he stampt his foot,
And from the basements deep to the high towers
Jarr'd his own golden region; and before
The quavering thunder thereupon had ceas'd,   225
His voice leapt out, despite of godlike curb,
To this result: "O dreams of day and night!
"O monstrous forms! O effigies of pain!
"O spectres busy in a cold, cold gloom!
"O lank-eared Phantoms of black-weeded pools!   230

Hinter V. 205 *hat* W.: Most like a rose bud to a faery's lute.
209 Yes, like a rose W.

"Why do I know ye? why have I seen ye? why
"Is my eternal essence thus distraught
"To see and to behold these horrors new?
"Saturn is fallen, am I too to fall?
"Am I to leave this haven of my rest, 235
"This cradle of my glory, this soft clime,
"This calm luxuriance of blissful light,
"These crystalline pavilions, and pure fanes,
"Of all my lucent empire? It is left
"Deserted, void, nor any haunt of mine. 240
"The blaze, the splendor, and the symmetry,
"I cannot see — but darkness, death and darkness.
"Even here, into my centre of repose,
"The shady visions come to domineer,
"Insult, and blind, and stifle up my pomp. — 245
"Fall! — No, by Tellus and her briny robes!
"Over the fiery frontier of my realms
"I will advance a terrible right arm
"Shall scare that infant thunderer, rebel Jove,
"And bid old Saturn take his throne again." — 250
He spake, and ceas'd, the while a heavier threat
Held struggle with his throat but came not forth;
For as in theatres of crowded men
Hubbub increases more they call out "Hush!"
So at Hyperion's words the Phantoms pale 255
Bestirr'd themselves, thrice horrible and cold;
And from the mirror'd level where he stood
A mist arose, as from a scummy marsh.
At this, through all his bulk an agony
Crept gradual, from the feet unto the crown, 260
Like a lithe serpent vast and muscular

Making slow way, with head and neck convuls'd
From over-strained might. Releas'd, he fled
To the eastern gates, and full six dewy hours
Before the dawn in season due should blush, 265
He breath'd fierce breath against the sleepy portals,
Clear'd them of heavy vapours, burst them wide
Suddenly on the ocean's chilly streams.
The planet orb of fire, whereon he rode
Each day from east to west the heavens through, 270
Spun round in sable curtaining of clouds:
Not therefore veiled quite, blindfold, and hid,
But ever and anon the glancing spheres,
Circles, and arcs, and broad-belting colure,
Glow'd through, and wrought upon the muffling dark 275
Sweet-shaped lightnings from the nadir deep
Up to the zenith, — hieroglyphics old,
Which sages and keen-eyed astrologers
Then living on the earth, with labouring thought
Won from the gaze of many centuries: 280
Now lost, save what we find on remnants huge
Of stone, or marble swart; their import gone,
Their wisdom long since fled. — Two wings this orb
Possess'd for glory, two fair argent wings,
Ever exalted at the God's approach: 285
And now, from forth the gloom their plumes immense
Rose, one by one, till all outspreaded were;

---

267 *Doppelpunkt hinter* wide *W.* 268 And, sudden *W.*
Komma hinter streams *W. Bei vv.* 277—280 *ein Strich und
qy in Blei am Rande, wahrscheinlich von des Dichters Hand,
mit Bezug auf die lockere logische Verknüpfung.*

While still the dazzling globe maintain'd eclipse,
Awaiting for Hyperion's command.
Fain would he have commanded, fain took throne   290
And bid the day begin, if but for change.
He might not: — No, though a primeval God:
The sacred seasons might not be disturb'd.
Therefore the operations of the dawn
Stay'd in their birth, even as here 'tis told.   295
Those silver wings expanded sisterly,
Eager to sail their orb; the porches wide
Open'd upon the dusk demesnes of night;
And the bright Titan, phrenzied with new woes,
Unus'd to bend, by hard compulsion bent   300
His spirit to the sorrow of the time;
And all along a dismal rack of clouds,
Upon the boundaries of day and night,
He stretch'd himself in grief and radiance faint.
There as he lay, the Heaven with its stars   305
Look'd down on him with pity, and the voice
Of Cœlus, from the universal space,
Thus whisper'd low and solemn in his ear.
"O brightest of my children dear, earth-born
"And sky-engendered, Son of Mysteries   310
"All unrevealed even to the powers
"Which met at thy creating; at whose joys
"And palpitations sweet, and pleasures soft,
"I, Cœlus, wonder, how they came and whence;
"And at the fruits thereof what shapes they be, 315
"Distinct, and visible; symbols divine,
"Manifestations of that beauteous life
"Diffus'd unseen throughout eternal space:

"Of these new-form'd art thou, oh brightest child!
"Of these, thy brethren and the Goddesses! 320
"There is sad feud among ye, and rebellion
"Of son against his sire. I saw him fall,
"I saw my first-born tumbled from his throne!
"To me his arms were spread, to me his voice
"Found way from forth the thunders round his head! 325
"Pale wox I, and in vapours hid my face.
"Art thou, too, near such doom? vague fear there is:
"For I have seen my sons most unlike Gods.
"Divine ye were created, and divine
"In sad demeanour, solemn, undisturb'd, 330
"Unruffled, like high Gods, ye liv'd and ruled:
"Now I behold in you fear, hope, and wrath:
"Actions of rage and passion: even as
"I see them, on the mortal world beneath,
"In men who die. — This is the grief, O Son! 335
"Sad sign of ruin, sudden dismay, and fall!
"Yet do thou strive; as thou art capable,
"As thou canst move about, an evident God;
"And canst oppose to each malignant hour
"Ethereal presence: — I am but a voice; 340
"My life is but the life of winds and tides,
"No more than winds and tides can I avail: —
"But thou canst. — Be thou therefore in the van
"Of circumstance; yea, seize the arrow's barb
"Before the tense string murmur. — To the earth! 345
"For there thou wilt find Saturn, and his woes.

---

319 f. *Die Wörter* these new-form'd *und* these, thy brethren sind bei W. unterstrichen; dazu am Rande ein *qy* in Blei, wohl vom Dichter selbst (vgl. 227). 332 ye st. you W.; vgl. 2, 327.

"Meantime I will keep watch on thy bright sun,
"And of thy seasons be a careful nurse." —
Ere half this region-whisper had come down,
Hyperion arose, and on the stars   350
Lifted his curved lids, and kept them wide
Until it ceas'd; and still he kept them wide:
And still they were the same bright, patient stars.
Then with a slow incline of his broad breast,
Like to a diver in the pearly seas,   355
Forward he stoop'd over the airy shore,
And plung'd all noiseless into the deep night.

HYPERION.

BOOK II.

JUST at the self-same beat of Time's wide wings
Hyperion slid into the rustled air,
And Saturn gain'd with Thea that sad place
Where Cybele and the bruised Titans mourn'd.
It was a den where no insulting light   5
Could glimmer on their tears; where their own groans
They felt, but heard not, for the solid roar
Of thunderous waterfalls and torrents hoarse,
Pouring a constant bulk, uncertain where.
Crag jutting forth to crag, and rocks that seem'd   10
Ever as if just rising from a sleep,
Forehead to forehead held their monstrous horns;
And thus in thousand hugest phantasies
Made a fit roofing to this nest of woe.
Instead of thrones, hard flint they sat upon,   15
Couches of rugged stone, and slaty ridge

Stubborn'd with iron. All were not assembled:
Some chain'd in torture, and some wandering.
Cœus, and Gyges, and Briareüs,
Typhon, and Dolor, and Porphyrion, 20
With many more, the brawniest in assault,
Were pent in regions of laborious breath:
Dungeon'd in opaque element, to keep
Their clenched teeth still clench'd, and all their limbs
Lock'd up like veins of metal, crampt and screw'd: 25
Without a motion, save of their big hearts
Heaving in pain, and horribly convuls'd
With sanguine feverous boiling gurge of pulse.
Mnemosyne was straying in the world;
Far from her moon had Phœbe wandered; 30
And many else were free to roam abroad,
But for the main, here found they covert drear.
Scarce images of life, one here, one there,
Lay vast and edgeways; like a dismal cirque
Of Druid stones, upon a forlorn moor, 35
When the chill rain begins at shut of eve,
In dull November, and their chancel vault,
The Heaven itself, is blinded throughout night.
Each one kept shroud, nor to his neighbour gave
Or word, or look, or action of despair. 40
Creüs was one; his ponderous iron mace
Lay by him, and a shatter'd rib of rock
Told of his rage, ere he thus sank and pined.
Jäpetus another; in his grasp,
A serpent's plashy neck; its barbed tongue 45
Squeez'd from the gorge, and all its uncurl'd length
Dead; and because the creature could not spit

Its poison in the eyes of conquering Jove.
Next Cottus: prone he lay, chin uppermost,
As though in pain: for still upon the flint   50
He ground severe his skull, with open mouth
And eyes at horrid working. Nearest him
Asia, born of most enormous Caf,
Who cost her mother Tellus keener pangs,
Though feminine, than any of her sons: 55
More thought than woe was in her dusky face,
For she was prophesying of her glory;
And in her wide imagination stood
Palm-shaded temples, and high rival fanes,
By Oxus or in Ganges' sacred isles.   60
Even as Hope upon her anchor leans,
So leant she, not so fair, upon a tusk
Shed from the broadest of her elephants.
Above her, on a crag's uneasy shelve,
Upon his elbow rais'd, all prostrate else,   65
Shadow'd Enceladus; once tame and mild
As grazing ox unworried in the meads;
Now tiger-passion'd, lion-thoughted, wroth,
He meditated, plotted, and even now
Was hurling mountains in that second war,   70
Not long delay'd, that scar'd the younger Gods
To hide themselves in forms of beast and bird.
Not far hence Atlas; and beside him prone
Phorcus, the sire of Gorgons. Neighbour'd close
Oceanus, and Tethys, in whose lap   75
Sobb'd Clymene among her tangled hair.

---

60 shaded isles *W.; wohl Versehen des Schreibers.*

In midst of all lay Themis, at the feet
Of Ops the queen all clouded round from sight;
No shape distinguishable, more than when
Thick night confounds the pine-tops with the clouds: 80
And many else whose names may not be told.
For when the Muse's wings are air-ward spread,
Who shall delay her flight? And she must chaunt
Of Saturn, and his guide, who now had climb'd
With damp and slippery footing from a depth 85
More horrid still. Above a sombre cliff
Their heads appear'd, and up their stature grew
Till on the level height their steps found ease:
Then Thea spread abroad her trembling arms
Upon the precincts of this nest of pain. 90
And sidelong fix'd her eye on Saturn's face:
There saw she direst strife; the supreme God
At war with all the frailty of grief,
Of rage, of fear, anxiety, revenge,
Remorse, spleen, hope, but most of all despair. 95
Against these plagues he strove in vain; for Fate
Had pour'd a mortal oil upon his head,
A disanointing poison; so that Thea,
Affrighted, kept her still, and let him pass
First onwards in, among the fallen tribe. 100

 As with us mortal men, the laden heart
Is persecuted more, and fever'd more,
When it is nighing to the mournful house
Where other hearts are sick of the same bruise:
So Saturn, as he walk'd into the midst, 105

---

89 arm *W*.

Felt faint, and would have sunk among the rest,
But that he met Enceladus's eye,
Whose mightiness, and awe of him, at once
Came like an inspiration; and he shouted,
"Titans, behold your God!" at which some groan'd;   110
Some started on their feet; some also shouted;
Some wept, some wail'd, all bow'd with reverence;
And Ops, uplifting her black folded veil,
Show'd her pale cheeks, and all her forehead wan,
Her eye-brows thin and jet, and hollow eyes.   115
There is a roaring in the bleak-grown pines
When Winter lifts his voice; there is a noise
Among immortals when a God gives sign,
With hushing finger, how he means to load
His tongue with the full weight of utterless thought,   120
With thunder, and with music, and with pomp:
Such noise is like the roar of bleak-grown pines;
Which, when it ceases in this mountain'd world,
No other sound succeeds; but ceasing here,
Among these fallen, Saturn's voice therefrom   125
Grew up like organ, that begins anew
Its strain, when other harmonies, stopt short,
Leave the dinn'd air vibrating silverly.
Thus grew it up — "Not in my own sad breast,
"Which is its own great judge and searcher out,   130
"Can I find reason why ye should be thus:
"Not in the legends of the first of days,
"Studied from that old spirit-leaved book

---

124 is heard *st.* succeeds *W.* 128 vibrated *W.*, *über ausradiertem* vibrating.

"Which starry Uranus with finger bright
"Sav'd from the shores of darkness, when the waves 135
"Low-ebb'd still hid it up in shallow gloom; —
"And the which book ye know I ever kept
"For my firm-based footstool: — Ah, infirm!
"Not there, nor in sign, symbol, or portent
"Of element, earth, water, air, and fire, — 140
"At war, at peace, or inter-quarreling
"One against one, or two, or three, or all
"Each several one against the other three.
"As fire with air loud warring when rain-floods
"Drown both, and press them both against earth's face. 145
"Where, finding sulphur, a quadruple wrath
"Unhinges the poor world; — not in that strife,
"Wherefrom I take strange lore, and read it deep,
"Can I find reason why ye should be thus:
"No, no-where can unriddle, though I search, 150
"And pore on Nature's universal scroll
"Even to swooning, why ye, Divinities,
"The first-born of all shap'd and palpable Gods,
"Should cower beneath what, in comparison,
"Is untremendous might. Yet ye are here, 155
"O'erwhelm'd, and spurn'd, and batter'd, ye are here!
"O Titans, shall I say, 'Arise!' — Ye groan:
"Shall I say 'Crouch!' — Ye groan. What can I then?
"O Heaven wide! O unseen parent dear!
"What can I? Tell me, all ye brethren Gods, 160
"How we can war, how engine our great wrath!
"O speak your counsel now, for Saturn's ear
"Is all a-hunger'd. Thou, Oceanus,

---

134 Which starr'd Uranus with his finger bright *W*.

"Ponderest high and deep; and in thy face
"I see, astonied, that severe content
"Which comes of thought and musing; give us help!"

So ended Saturn; and the God of the Sea,
Sophist and sage, from no Athenian grove,
But cogitation in his watery shades,
Arose, with locks not oozy, and began,
In murmurs, which his first-endeavouring tongue
Caught infant-like from the far-foamed sands.
"O ye, whom wrath consumes! who, passion-stung,
"Writhe at defeat, and nurse your agonies!
"Shut up your senses, stifle up your ears,
"My voice is not a bellows unto ire.
"Yet listen, ye who will, whilst I bring proof
"How ye, perforce, must be content to stoop:
"And in the proof much comfort will I give,
"If ye will take that comfort in its truth.
"We fall by course of Nature's law, not force
"Of thunder, or of Jove. Great Saturn, thou
"Hast sifted well the atom-universe;
"But for this reason, that thou art the King,
"And only blind from sheer supremacy,
"One avenue was shaded from thine eyes,
"Through which I wandered to eternal truth.
"And first, as thou wast not the first of powers,
"So art thou not the last; it cannot be:
"Thou art not the beginning nor the end.
"From chaos and parental darkness came
"Light, the first fruits of that intestine broil,
"That sullen ferment, which for wondrous ends

"Was ripening in itself. The ripe hour came,
"And with it light, and light, engendering   195
"Upon its own producer, forthwith touch'd
"The whole enormous matter into life.
"Upon that very hour, our parentage,
"The Heavens and the Earth, were manifest:
"Then thou first-born, and we the giant-race,   200
"Found ourselves ruling new and beauteous realms.
"Now comes the pain of truth, to whom 'tis pain;
"O folly! for to bear all naked truths,
"And to envisage circumstance, all calm,
"That is the top of sovereignty. Mark well!   205
"As Heaven and Earth are fairer, fairer far
"Than Chaos and blank Darkness, though once chiefs;
"And as we show beyond that Heaven and Earth
"In form and shape compact and beautiful,
"In will, in action free, companionship,   210
"And thousand other signs of purer life;
"So on our heels a fresh perfection treads,
"A power more strong in beauty, born of us
"And fated to excel us, as we pass
"In glory that old Darkness: nor are we   215
"Thereby more conquer'd, than by us the rule
"Of shapeless Chaos. Say, doth the dull soil
"Quarrel with the proud forests it hath fed,
"And feedeth still, more comely than itself?
"Can it deny the chiefdom of green groves?   220
"Or shall the tree be envious of the dove
"Because it cooeth, and hath snowy wings
"To wander wherewithal and find its joys?
"We are such forest-trees, and our fair boughs

"Have bred forth, not pale solitary doves, 225
"But eagles golden-feather'd, who do tower
"Above us in their beauty, and must reign
"In right thereof: for 'tis the eternal law
"That first in beauty should be first in might:
"Yea, by that law, another race may drive 230
"Our conquerors to mourn as we do now.
"Have ye beheld the young God of the Seas,
"My dispossessor? Have ye seen his face?
"Have ye beheld his chariot, foam'd along
"By noble winged creatures he hath made? 235
"I saw him on the calmed waters scud,
"With such a glow of beauty in his eyes,
"That it enforc'd me to bid sad farewell
"To all my empire: farewell sad I took,
"And hither came, to see how dolorous fate 240
"Had wrought upon ye: and how I might best
"Give consolation in this woe extreme.
"Receive the truth, and let it be your balm."

Whether through poz'd conviction, or disdain,
They guarded silence, when Oceanus 245
Left murmuring, what deepest thought can tell?
But so it was, none answer'd for a space,
Save one whom none regarded, Clymene;
And yet she answer'd not, only complain'd,
With hectic lips, and eyes up-looking mild, 250
Thus wording timidly among the fierce:
"O Father, I am here the simplest voice,
"And all my knowledge is that joy is gone,
"And this thing woe crept in among our hearts,

"There to remain for ever, as I fear: 255
"I would not bode of evil, if I thought
"So weak a creature could turn off the help
"Which by just right should come of mighty Gods;
"Yet let me tell my sorrow, let me tell
"Of what I heard, and how it made me weep. 260
"And know that we had parted from all hope.
"I stood upon a shore, a pleasant shore,
"Where a sweet clime was breathed from a land
"Of fragrance, quietness, and trees, and flowers.
"Full of calm joy it was, as I of grief; 265
"Too full of joy and soft delicious warmth;
"So that I felt a movement in my heart
"To chide, and to reproach that solitude
"With songs of misery, music of our woes;
"And sat me down, and took a mouthed shell 270
"And murmur'd into it, and made melody —
"O melody no more! for while I sang,
"And with poor skill let pass into the breeze
"The dull shell's echo, from a bowery strand
"Just opposite, an island of the sea. 275
"There came enchantment with the shifting wind,
"That did both drown and keep alive my ears.
"I threw my shell away upon the sand,
"And a wave fill'd it, as my sense was fill'd
"With that new blissful golden melody. 280
"A living death was in each gush of sounds,
"Each family of rapturous hurried notes,
"That fell, one after one, yet all at once,
"Like pearl beads dropping sudden from their string:
"And then another, then another strain, 285

"Each like a dove leaving its olive perch,
"With music wing'd instead of silent plumes,
"To hover round my head, and make me sick
"Of joy and grief at once. Grief overcame,
"And I was stopping up my frantic ears, 290
"When, past all hindrance of my trembling hands,
"A voice came sweeter, sweeter than all tune,
"And still it cried, 'Apollo! young Apollo!
"'The morning-bright Apollo! young Apollo!'
"I fled, it follow'd me, and cried 'Apollo!' 295
"O Father, and O Brethren, had ye felt
"Those pains of mine; O Saturn, hadst thou felt,
"Ye would not call this too indulged tongue
"Presumptuous, in thus venturing to be heard."

So far her voice flow'd on, like timorous brook 300
That, lingering along a pebbled coast,
Doth fear to meet the sea: but sea it met,
And shudder'd; for the overwhelming voice
Of huge Enceladus swallow'd it in wrath:
The ponderous syllables, like sullen waves 305
In the half-glutted hollows of reef-rocks,
Came booming thus, while still upon his arm
He lean'd; not rising, from supreme contempt.
"Or shall we listen to the over-wise,
"Or to the over-foolish giant, Gods? 310
"Not thunderbolt on thunderbolt, till all
"That rebel Jove's whole armoury were spent,
"Not world on world upon these shoulders piled,
"Could agonize me more than baby-words

---
312 was *W.* 313 pour'd *st.* piled *W.*

"In midst of this dethronement horrible. 315
"Speak! roar! shout! yell! ye sleepy Titans all.
"Do ye forget the blows, the buffets vile?
"Are ye not smitten by a youngling arm?
"Dost thou forget, sham Monarch of the Waves,
"Thy scalding in the seas? What, have I rous'd 320
"Your spleens with so few simple words as these?
"O joy! for now I see ye are not lost:
"O joy! for now I see a thousand eyes
"Wide glaring for revenge!" — As this he said,
He lifted up his stature vast, and stood, 325
Still without intermission speaking thus:
"Now ye are flames, I'll tell you how to burn,
"And purge the ether of our enemies:
"How to feed fierce the crooked stings of fire,
"And singe away the swollen clouds of Jove, 330
"Stifling that puny essence in its tent.
"O let him feel the evil he hath done;
"For though I scorn Oceanus's lore,
"Much pain have I for more than loss of realms:
"The days of peace and slumberous calm are fled; 335
"Those days, all innocent of scathing war,
"When all the fair Existences of heaven
"Came open-eyed to guess what we would speak: —
"That was before our brows were taught to frown,
"Before our lips knew else but solemn sounds; 340
"That was before we knew the winged thing,
"Victory, might be lost, or might be won.
"And be ye mindful that Hyperion,

---

327 tell ye *W.; cgl. l. 332.*

"Our brightest brother, still is undisgraced —
"Hyperion, lo! his radiance is here!" 345

 All eyes were on Enceladus's face,
And they beheld, while still Hyperion's name
Flew from his lips up to the vaulted rocks,
A pallid gleam across his features stern:
Not savage, for he saw full many a God 350
Wroth as himself. He look'd upon them all,
And in each face he saw a gleam of light,
But splendider in Saturn's, whose hoar locks
Shone like the bubbling foam about a keel
When the prow sweeps into a midnight cove. 355
In pale and silver silence they remain'd,
Till suddenly a splendour, like the morn,
Pervaded all the beetling gloomy steeps,
All the sad spaces of oblivion,
And every gulf, and every chasm old, 360
And every height, and every sullen depth,
Voiceless, or hoarse with loud tormented streams:
And all the everlasting cataracts,
And all the headlong torrents far and near,
Mantled before in darkness and huge shade, 365
Now saw the light and made it terrible.
It was Hyperion: — a granite peak
His bright feet touch'd, and there he stay'd to view
The misery his brilliance had betray'd
To the most hateful seeing of itself. 370
Golden his hair of short Numidian curl,
Regal his shape majestic, a vast shade
In midst of his own brightness, like the bulk

Of Memnon's image at the set of sun
To one who travels from the dusking East: 375
Sighs, too, as mournful as that Memnon's harp
He utter'd, while his hands contemplative
He press'd together, and in silence stood.
Despondence seiz'd again the fallen Gods
At sight of the dejected King of Day, 380
And many hid their faces from the light:
But fierce Enceladus sent forth his eyes
Among the brotherhood; and, at their glare,
Uprose Jäpetus, and Creüs too,
And Phorcus, sea-born, and together strode 385
To where he towered on his eminence.
There those four shouted forth old Saturn's name;
Hyperion from the peak loud answered, "Saturn!"
Saturn sat near the Mother of the Gods,
In whose face was no joy, though all the Gods 390
Gave from their hollow throats the name of "Saturn!"

HYPERION.

BOOK III.

Thus in alternate uproar and sad peace,
Amazed were those Titans utterly.
O leave them, Muse! O leave them to their woes;
For thou art weak to sing such tumults dire:
A solitary sorrow best befits   5
Thy lips, and antheming a lonely grief.
Leave them, O Muse! for thou anon wilt find
Many a fallen old Divinity
Wandering in vain about bewildered shores.
Meantime touch piously the Delphic harp,   10
And not a wind of heaven but will breathe
In aid soft warble from the Dorian flute;
For lo! 'tis for the Father of all verse.
Flush every thing that hath a vermeil hue,
Let the rose glow intense and warm the air,   15
And let the clouds of even and of morn

Float in voluptuous fleeces o'er the hills;
Let the red wine within the goblet boil,
Cold as a bubbling well: let faint-lipp'd shells,
On sands, or in great deeps, vermilion turn   20
Through all their labyrinths; and let the maid
Blush keenly, as with some warm kiss surpris'd.
Chief isle of the embowered Cyclades,
Rejoice, O Delos, with thine olives green,
And poplars, and lawn-shading palms, and beech,   25
In which the Zephyr breathes the loudest song,
And hazels thick, dark-stemm'd beneath the shade:
Apollo is once more the golden theme!
Where was he, when the Giant of the Sun
Stood bright, amid the sorrow of his peers?   30
Together had he left his mother fair
And his twin-sister sleeping in their bower,
And in the morning twilight wandered forth
Beside the osiers of a rivulet,
Full ankle-deep in lilies of the vale.   35
The nightingale had ceas'd, and a few stars
Were lingering in the heavens, while the thrush
Began calm-throated. Throughout all the isle
There was no covert, no retired cave
Unhaunted by the murmurous noise of waves,   40
Though scarcely heard in many a green recess.
He listen'd, and he wept, and his bright tears
Went trickling down the golden bow he held.
Thus with half-shut suffused eyes he stood,
While from beneath some cumbrous boughs hard by 45
With solemn step an awful Goddess came,
And there was purport in her looks for him,

Which he with eager guess began to read
Perplex'd, the while melodiously he said:
"How cam'st thou over the unfooted sea? 50
"Or hath that antique mien and robed form
"Mov'd in these vales invisible till now?
"Sure I have heard those vestments sweeping o'er
"The fallen leaves, when I have sat alone
"In cool mid-forest. Surely I have traced 55
"The rustle of those ample skirts about
"These grassy solitudes, and seen the flowers
"Lift up their heads, as still the whisper pass'd.
"Goddess! I have beheld those eyes before,
"And their eternal calm, and all that face, 60
"Or I have dream'd." — "Yes", said the supreme shape,
"Thou hast dream'd of me; and awaking up
"Didst find a lyre all golden by thy side,
"Whose strings touch'd by thy fingers, all the vast
"Unwearied ear of the whole universe 65
"Listen'd in pain and pleasure at the birth
"Of such new tuneful wonder. Is't not strange
"That thou shouldst weep, so gifted? Tell me, youth,
"What sorrow thou canst feel; for I am sad
"When thou dost shed a tear: explain thy griefs 70
"To one who in this lonely isle hath been
"The watcher of thy sleep and hours of life,
"From the young day when first thy infant hand
„Pluck'd witless the weak flowers, till thine arm
"Could bend that bow heroic to all times. 75
"Show thy heart's secret to an ancient Power

---

49 and while W.

"Who hath forsaken old and sacred thrones
"For prophecies of thee, and for the sake
"Of loveliness new born." — Apollo then,
With sudden scrutiny and gloomless eyes, 80
Thus answer'd, while his white melodious throat
Throbb'd with the syllables. — "Mnemosyne!
"Thy name is on my tongue, I know not how:
"Why should I tell thee what thou so well seest?
"Why should I strive to show what from thy lips 85
"Would come no mystery? For me, dark, dark,
"And painful vile oblivion seals my eyes:
"I strive to search wherefore I am so sad,
"Until a melancholy numbs my limbs;
"And then upon the grass I sit, and moan, 90
"Like one who once had wings. — O why should I
"Feel curs'd and thwarted, when the liegeless air
"Yields to my step aspirant? why should I
"Spurn the green turf as hateful to my feet?
"Goddess benign, point forth some unknown thing: 95
"Are there not other regions than this isle?
"What are the stars? There is the sun, the sun!
"And the most patient brilliance of the moon!
"And stars by thousands! Point me out the way
"To any one particular beauteous star, 100
"And I will flit into it with my lyre,
"And make its silvery splendour pant with bliss.
"I have heard the cloudy thunder: Where is power?
"Whose hand, whose essence, what divinity
"Makes this alarum in the elements, 105
"While I here idle listen on the shores
"In fearless yet in aching ignorance?

"O tell me, lonely Goddess, by thy harp,
"That waileth every morn and eventide,
"Tell me why thus I rave, about these groves! 110
"Mute thou remainest — Mute! yet I can read
"A wondrous lesson in thy silent face:
"Knowledge enormous makes a God of me.
"Names, deeds, gray legends, dire events, rebellions,
"Majesties, sovran voices, agonies, 115
"Creations and destroyings, all at once
"Pour into the wide hollows of my brain,
"And deify me, as if some blithe wine
"Or bright elixir peerless I had drunk,
"And so become immortal." — Thus the God, 120
While his enkindled eyes, with level glance
Beneath his white soft temples, stedfast kept
Trembling with light upon Mnemosyne.
Soon wild commotions shook him, and made flush
All the immortal fairness of his limbs; 125
Most like the struggle at the gate of death;
Or liker still to one who should take leave
Of pale immortal death, and with a pang

---

125 W. hat ein Komma hinter limbs, und es folgen drei beseitigte Verse:

    Into a hue more roseate than sweet pain
    Gives to a ravish'd nymph, when her warm tears
    Gush luscious with no sob; or more severe;
    More like the struggle etc.

Mit Bleistift gestrichen, wahrscheinlich von Keats selbst (s. Einleitung S. 40).　126 More st. Most W., mit Blei durchstrichen und am Rande And, vermutlich von Woodhouse's Hand. Die Bleistriche sind von denen in den drei vorhergehenden Zeilen verschieden.

As hot as death's is chill, with fierce convulse
Die into life: so young Apollo anguish'd: 130
His very hair, his golden tresses famed
Kept undulation round his eager neck.
During the pain Mnemosyne upheld
Her arms as one who prophesied. — At length
Apollo shriek'd: — and lo! from all his limbs 135
Celestial * * * * * *
* * * * * * * *

---

131 *Der Schreiber hat* fam'd, *von Woodhouse verbessert in* fann'd; *aber der Dichter schrieb offenbar* fam'd *bezw.* famed.   132 Keep *W*.   136 *Bei W. ist der letzte Vers mit Bleistift von des Dichters eigener Hand so ergänzt:*
Celestial Glory dawn'd. he was a god!
Statt dawn'd *zuerst* brake: *durchstrichen. Auch die Worte* he was a god *sind wieder ausgestrichen. Vgl. Forman KW 1, S. XLIX.*

HYPERION, A VISION.

Versuch einer Überarbeitung des Gedichts.

HYPERION, A VISION.

FANATICS have their dreams, wherewith they weave
A paradise for a sect; the savage, too,
From forth the loftiest fashion of his sleep
Guesses at heaven: pity these have not
Traced upon vellum or wild Indian leaf   5
The shadows of melodious utterance,
But bare of laurel they live, dream, and die;
For Poesy alone can tell her dreams, —
With the fine spell of words alone can save
Imagination from the sable chain   10
And dumb enchantment. Who alive can say,
"Thou art no Poet — may'st not tell thy dreams?"
Since every man whose soul is not a clod
Hath visions and would speak, if he had loved,
And been well nurtured in his mother tongue.   15
Whether the dream now purposed to rehearse

H.¹ = Houghton's Text in den Miscellanies der Philobiblon Society, vol. III. (1856—57). H.² = Houghton's 2. Ausgabe im Anhang der 2. Aufl. des Life and Letters (1867). F. = Forman's Text in der 2. Aufl. seiner Gesamtausg. v. Keats' Werken (1889). 5 ff. Im Ms. schwerlich schon Verszählung. H.¹,² numeriert nur jeden zehnten Vers.

Be poet's or fanatic's will be known
When this warm scribe, my hand, is in the grave.

    Methought I stood where trees of every clime,
Palm, myrtle, oak, and sycamore, and beech,   20
With plantane and spice-blossoms, made a screen,
In neighbourhood of fountains (by the noise
Soft-showering in mine ears), and (by the touch
Of scent) not far from roses. Twining round
I saw an arbour with a drooping roof   25
Of trellis vines, and bells, and larger blooms,
Like floral censers, swinging light in air;
Before its wreathed doorway, on a mound
Of moss, was spread a feast of summer fruits,
Which, nearer seen, seem'd refuse of a meal   30
By angel tasted or our Mother Eve;
For empty shells were scatter'd on the grass,
And grapestalks but half-bare, and remnants more
Sweet-smelling, whose pure kinds I could not know.
Still was more plenty than the fabled horn   35
Thrice emptied could pour forth at banqueting,
For Proserpine return'd to her own fields,
Where the white heifers low. And appetite,
More yearning than on earth I ever felt,
Growing within, I ate deliciously, —   40
And, after not long, thirsted; for thereby
Stood a cool vessel of transparent juice
Sipp'd by the wander'd bee, the which I took,
And pledging all the mortals of the world,
And all the dead whose names are in our lips,   45
Drank. That full draught is parent of my theme.

No Asian poppy nor elixir fine
Of the soon-fading, jealous, Caliphat,
No poison gender'd in close monkish cell,
To thin the scarlet conclave of old men, 50
Could so have rapt unwilling life away.
Among the fragrant husks and berries crush'd
Upon the grass, I struggled hard against
The domineering potion, but in vain.
The cloudy swoon came on, and down I sank, 55
Like a Silenus on an antique vase.
How long I slumber'd 'tis a chance to guess.
When sense of life return'd, I started up
As if with wings, but the fair trees were gone,
The mossy mound and arbour were no more: 60
I look'd around upon the curved sides
Of an old sanctuary, with roof august,
Builded so high, it seem'd that filmed clouds
Might spread beneath as o'er the stars of heaven.
So old the place was, I remember'd none 65
The like upon the earth: what I had seen
Of gray cathedrals, buttress'd walls, rent towers,
The superannuations of sunk realms,
Or Nature's rocks toil'd hard in waves and winds,
Seem'd but the faulture of decrepit things 70
To that eternal domed monument.
Upon the marble at my feet there lay
Store of strange vessels and large draperies,
Which needs had been of dyed asbestos wove
Or in that place the moth could not corrupt, 75
So white the linen, so, in some, distinct
Ran imageries from a sombre loom.

All in a mingled heap confused there lay
Robes, golden tongs, censer and chafing-dish,
Girdles, and chains, and holy jewelries. 80

    Turning from these with awe, once more I raised
My eyes to fathom the space every way:
The embossed roof, the silent massy range
Of columns north and south, ending in mist
Of nothing; then to eastward, where black gates 85
Were shut against the sunrise evermore;
Then to the west I look'd, and saw far off
An image, huge of feature as a cloud.
At level of whose feet an altar slept,
To be approach'd on either side by steps 90
And marble balustrade, and patient travail
To count with toil the innumerable degrees.
Towards the altar sober-paced I went,
Repressing haste as too unholy there;
And, coming nearer, saw beside the shrine 95
One ministering; and there arose a flame.
When in midday the sickening east-wind
Shifts sudden to the south, the small warm rain
Melts out the frozen incense from all flowers,
And fills the air with so much pleasant health 100
That even the dying man forgets his shroud;—
Even so that lofty sacrificial fire,
Sending forth Maian incense, spread around

---

  83 emboss'd *H.*[1]; embossed *H.*[2] und *F.*   96 *H.*[1,2] hat einen Punkt hinter flame; *F.* hat gar keine Interpunktion (auch in der neuesten Aufl. seiner kleinen Ausg. nicht).
97 As *st.* When *H.*[1]; When *H.*[2], *F.*

Forgetfulness of everything but bliss,
And clouded all the altar with soft smoke;   105
From whose white fragrant curtains thus I heard
Language pronounced: "If thou canst not ascend
These steps, die on that marble where thou art.
Thy flesh, near cousin to the common dust,
Will parch for lack of nutriment; thy bones   110
Will wither in few years, and vanish so
That not the quickest eye could find a grain
Of what thou now art on that pavement cold.
The sands of thy short life are spent this hour,
And no hand in the universe can turn   115
Thy hourglass, if these gummed leaves be burnt
Ere thou canst mount up these immortal steps."
I heard, I look'd: two senses both at once,
So fine, so subtle, felt the tyranny
Of that fierce threat and the hard task proposed.   120
Prodigious seem'd the toil; the leaves were yet
Burning, when suddenly a palsied chill
Struck from the paved level up my limbs,
And was ascending quick to put cold grasp
Upon those streams that pulse beside the throat.   125
I shriek'd, and the sharp anguish of my shriek
Stung my own ears; I strove hard to escape
The numbness, strove to gain the lowest step.
Slow, heavy, deadly was my pace: the cold
Grew stifling, suffocating at the heart;   130
And when I clasp'd my hands I felt them not.
One minute before death my iced foot touch'd

---

116 gumm'd *H.*¹ *(!)*; gummed *H.*². *F.*

The lowest stair; and, as it touch'd, life seem'd
To pour in at the toes; I mounted up
As once fair angels on a ladder flew   135
From the green turf to heaven. "Holy Power",
Cried I, approaching near the horned shrine.
"What am I that should so be saved from death?
What am I that another death come not
To choke my utterance, sacrilegious, here?"   140
Then said the veiled shadow: "Thou hast felt
What 'tis to die and live again before
Thy fated hour; that thou hadst power to do so
Is thine own safety; thou hast dated on
Thy doom." "High Prophetess", said I, "purge off, 145
Benign, if so it please thee, my mind's film."
"None can usurp this height", returned that shade,
"But those to whom the miseries of the world
Are misery, and will not let them rest.
All else who find a haven in the world,   150
Where they may thoughtless sleep away their days,
If by a chance into this fane they come,
Rot on the pavement where thou rottedst half."
"Are there not thousands in the world", said I,
Encouraged by the sooth voice of the shade,   155
"Who love their fellows even to the death,
Who feel the giant agony of the world,
And more, like slaves to poor humanity,
Labour for mortal good? I sure should see
Other men here, but I am here alone."   160
"Those whom thou spakest of are no visionaries",
Rejoin'd that voice; "they are no dreamers weak;
They seek no wonder but the human face,

No music but a happy-noted voice:
They come not here, they have no thought to come; 165
And thou art here, for thou art less than they.
What benefit canst thou do, or all thy tribe,
To the great world? Thou art a dreaming thing,
A fever of thyself: think of the earth;
What bliss, even in hope, is there for thee? 170
What haven? every creature hath its home,
Every sole man hath days of joy and pain,
Whether his labours be sublime or low —
The pain alone, the joy alone, distinct:
Only the dreamer venoms all his days, 175
Bearing more woe than all his sins deserve.
Therefore, that happiness be somewhat shared,
Such things as thou art are admitted oft
Into like gardens thou didst pass erewhile,
And suffer'd in these temples: for that cause 180
Thou standest safe beneath this statue's knees."
"That I am favour'd for unworthiness,
By such propitious parley medicined
In sickness not ignoble, I rejoice,
Aye, and could weep for love of such award." 185
So answer'd I, continuing, "If it please,
Majestic shadow, tell me where I am,
Whose altar this, for whom this incense curls;
What image this whose face I cannot see
For the broad marble knees; and who thou art, 190
Of accent feminine, so courteous?"

    Then the tall shade, in drooping linen veil'd,
Spoke out, so much more earnest, that her breath

Stirr'd the thin folds of gauze that drooping hung
About a golden censer from her hand   195
Pendent; and by her voice I knew she shed
Long-treasured tears. "This temple, sad and lone,
Is all spared from the thunder of a war
Foughten long since by giant hierarchy
Against rebellion; this old image here,   200
Whose carved features wrinkled as he fell,
Is Saturn's; I, Moneta, left supreme,
Sole goddess of this desolation."
I had no words to answer, for my tongue,
Useless, could find about its roofed home   205
No syllable of a fit majesty
To make rejoinder to Moneta's mourn:
There was a silence, while the altar's blaze
Was fainting for sweet food. I look'd thereon,
And on the paved floor, where nigh were piled   210
Faggots of cinnamon, and many heaps
Of other crisped spicewood: then again
I look'd upon the altar, and its horns
Whiten'd with ashes, and its languorous flame,
And then upon the offerings again;   215
And so, by turns, till sad Moneta cried:
"The sacrifice is done, but not the less
Will I be kind to thee for thy good will.
My power, which to me is still a curse,
Shall be to thee a wonder; for the scenes   220
Still swooning vivid through my globed brain,
With an electral changing misery,
Thou shalt with these dull mortal eyes behold
Free from all pain, if wonder pain thee not."

As near as an immortal's sphered words   225
Could to a mother's soften were these last:
And yet I had a terror of her robes,
And chiefly of the veils that from her brow
Hung pale, and curtain'd her in mysteries,
That made my heart too small to hold its blood.   230
This saw that Goddess, and with sacred hand
Parted the veils. Then saw I a wan face,
Not pined by human sorrows, but bright-blanch'd
By an immortal sickness which kills not;
It works a constant change, which happy death   235
Can put no end to; deathwards progressing
To no death was that visage; it had past
The lily and the snow; and beyond these
I must not think now, though I saw that face.
But for her eyes I should have fled away;   240
They held me back with a benignant light,
Soft, mitigated by divinest lids
Half-closed, and visionless entire they seem'd
Of all external things; they saw me not,
But in blank splendour beam'd, like the mild moon,   245
Who comforts those she sees not, who knows not
What eyes are upward cast. As I had found
A grain of gold upon a mountain's side,
And, twinged with avarice, strain'd out my eyes
To search its sullen entrails rich with ore,   250
So, at the view of sad Moneta's brow,
I asked to see what things the hollow brow
Behind environed: what high tragedy
In the dark secret chambers of her skull
Was acting, that could give so dread a stress   255

To her cold lips, and fill with such a light
Her planetary eyes, and touch her voice
With such a sorrow? "Shade of Memory!"
Cried I, with act adorant at her feet,
"By all the gloom hung round thy fallen house, 260
By this last temple, by the golden age,
By great Apollo, thy dear foster-child,
And by thyself, forlorn divinity,
The pale Omega of a wither'd race,
Let me behold, according as thou saidst, 265
What in thy brain so ferments to and fro!"
No sooner had this conjuration past
My devout lips, than side by side we stood
(Like a stunt bramble by a solemn pine)
Deep in the shady sadness of a vale 270
Far sunken from the healthy breath of morn,
Far from the fiery noon and eve's one star.
Onward I look'd beneath the gloomy boughs,
And saw what first I thought an image huge,
Like to the image pedestall'd so high 275
In Saturn's temple; then Moneta's voice
Came brief upon mine ear. "So Saturn sat
When he had lost his realms;" whereon there grew
A power within me of enormous ken
To see as a god sees, and take the depth 280
Of things as nimbly as the outward eye
Can size and shape pervade. The lofty theme
Of those few words hung vast before my mind
With half-unravell'd web. I sat myself
Upon an eagle's watch, that I might see, 285
And seeing ne'er forget. No stir of life

Was in this shrouded vale, — not so much air
As in the zoning of a summer's day;
Robs not one light seed from the feathered grass:
But where the dead leaf fell there did it rest.　290
A stream went noiseless by, still deaden'd more
By reason of the fallen divinity
Spreading more shade; the Naiad 'mid her reeds
Prest her cold finger closer to her lips.

Along the margin-sand large foot-marks went　295
No further than to where old Saturn's feet
Had rested, and there slept how long a sleep!
Degraded, cold, upon the sodden ground
His old right hand lay nerveless, listless, dead,
Unsceptred, and his realmless eyes were closed;　300
While his bow'd head seem'd listening to the Earth,
His ancient mother, for some comfort yet.

It seem'd no force could wake him from his place;
But there came one who, with a kindred hand,
Touch'd his wide shoulders, after bending low　305
With reverence, though to one who knew it not.
Then came the grieved voice of Mnemosyne,
And grieved I hearken'd. "That divinity
Whom thou saw'st step from yon forlornest wood,
And with slow pace approach our fallen king,　310
Is Thea, softest-natured of our brood."
I mark'd the Goddess, in fair statuary
Surpassing wan Moneta by the head,
And in her sorrow nearer woman's tears.
There was a list'ning fear in her regard,　315
As if calamity had but begun;

As if the venomed clouds of evil days
Had spent their malice, and the sullen rear
Was with its stored thunder labouring up.
One hand she press'd upon that aching spot   320
Where beats the human heart, as if just there,
Though an immortal, she felt cruel pain;
The other upon Saturn's bended neck
She laid, and to the level of his ear
Leaning, with parted lips some words she spoke   325
In solemn tenour and deep organ-tone;
Some mourning words, which in our feeble tongue
Would come in this like accenting; how frail
To that large utterance of the early gods!

  "Saturn, look up! and for what, poor lost king?   330
I have no comfort for thee; no, not one;
I cannot say, wherefore thus sleepest thou?
For Heaven is parted from thee, and the Earth
Knows thee not, so afflicted, for a god.
The Ocean, too, with all its solemn noise,   335
Has from thy sceptre pass'd; and all the air
Is emptied of thy hoary majesty.
Thy thunder, captious at the new command,
Rumbles reluctant o'er our fallen house;
And thy sharp lightning, in unpractised hands,   340
Scourges and burns our once serene domain.

  With such remorseless speed still come new woes,
That unbelief has not a space to breathe.
Saturn! sleep on: me thoughtless, why should I
Thus violate thy slumbrous solitude?   345

---

345 slumber's *H.*¹; slumbrous *H.*². *F: so auch Hyp.* 1,49.

Why should I ope thy melancholy eyes?
Saturn! sleep on, while at thy feet I weep."

 As when upon a tranced summer-night
Forests, branch-charmed by the earnest stars,
Dream, and so dream all night without a noise,   350
Save from one gradual solitary gust
Swelling upon the silence, dying off,
As if the ebbing air had but one wave,
So came these words and went; the while in tears
She prest her fair large forehead to the earth,   355
Just where her fallen hair might spread in curls
A soft and silken net for Saturn's feet.
Long, long these two were postured motionless,
Like sculpture builded-up upon the grave
Of their own power. A long awful time   360
I look'd upon them: still they were the same;
The frozen God still bending to the earth,
And the sad Goddess weeping at his feet;
Moneta silent. Without stay or prop
But my own weak mortality, I bore   365
The load of this eternal quietude,
The unchanging gloom and the three fixed shapes
Ponderous upon my senses, a whole moon;
For by my burning brain I measured sure
Her silver seasons shedded on the night,   370
And every day by day methought I grew
More gaunt and ghostly. Oftentimes I pray'd
Intense, that death would take me from the vale

---

356 *F. setzt hinter* curls *ein Komma, das bei* H.[1,2] *fehlt.*

And all its burthens; gasping with despair
Of change, hour after hour I cursed myself, 375
Until old Saturn raised his faded eyes,
And look'd around and saw his kingdom gone,
And all the gloom and sorrow of the place,
And that fair kneeling goddess at his feet.

   As the moist scent of flowers, and grass, and leaves 380
Fills forest-dells with a pervading air,
Known to the woodland nostril, so the words
Of Saturn fill'd the mossy glooms around,
Even to the hollows of time-eaten oaks,
And to the windings of the foxes' hole, 385
With sad, low tones, while thus he spoke, and sent
Strange moanings to the solitary Pan.
"Moan, brethren, moan, for we are swallow'd up
And buried from all godlike exercise
Of influence benign on planets pale, 390
And peaceful sway upon man's harvesting,
And all those acts which Deity supreme
Doth ease its heart of love in. Moan and wail;
Moan, brethren, moan; for lo, the rebel spheres
Spin round; the stars their ancient courses keep; 395
Clouds still with shadowy moisture haunt the earth,
Still suck their fill of light from sun and moon;
Still buds the tree, and still the seashores murmur;
There is no death in all the universe,
No smell of death.—There shall be death. Moan, moan; 400
Moan, Cybele, moan; for thy pernicious babes
Have changed a god into an aching palsy.
Moan, brethren, moan, for I have no strength left;

Weak as the reed, weak, feeble as my voice.
Oh! Oh! the pain, the pain of feebleness: 405
Moan, moan, for still I thaw; or give me help;
Throw down those imps, and give me victory.
Let me hear other groans, and trumpets blown
Of triumph calm, and hymns of festival,
From the gold peaks of heaven's high-piled clouds; 410
Voices of soft proclaim, and silver stir
Of strings in hollow shells; and there shall be
Beautiful things made new, for the surprise
Of the sky-children." So he feebly ceased,
With such a poor and sickly-sounding pause, 415
Methought I heard some old man of the earth
Bewailing earthly loss; nor could my eyes
And ears act with that unison of sense
Which marries sweet sound with the grace of form,
And dolorous accent from a tragic harp 420
With large-limb'd visions. More I scrutinized.
Still fixt he sat beneath the sable trees,
Whose arms spread straggling in wild serpent forms,
With leaves all hush'd; his awful presence there
(Now all was silent) gave a deadly lie 425
To what I erewhile heard: only his lips
Trembled amid the white curls of his beard;
They told the truth, though round the snowy locks
Hung nobly, as upon the face of heaven
A mid-day fleece of clouds. Thea arose, 430
And stretcht her white arm through the hollow dark,
Pointing some whither: whereat he too rose,

---

416 heard *F.*; *H.*¹·² hear, *wohl ein Schreibfehler.*

Like a vast giant, seen by men at sea
To grow pale from the waves at dull midnight.
They melted from my sight into the woods; 435
Ere I could turn, Moneta cried, "These twain
Are speeding to the families of grief,
Where, rooft in by black rocks, they waste in pain
And darkness, for no hope." And she spake on,
As ye may read who can unwearied pass 440
Onward from the antechamber of this dream,
Where, even at the open doors, awhile
I must delay, and glean my memory
Of her high phrase — perhaps no further dare.

END OF CANTO I.

---

438 waste [wait?] *H*^{1,2}: waste *F*.

CANTO II.

"Mortal, that thou mayst understand aright,
I humanize my sayings to thine ear,
Making comparisons of earthly things;
Or thou mightst better listen to the wind,
Whose language is to thee a barren noise,   5
Though it blows legend-laden thro' the trees.
In melancholy realms big tears are shed,
More sorrow like to this, and such like woe,
Too huge for mortal tongue or pen of scribe.
The Titans fierce, self-hid or prison-bound,   10
Groan for the old allegiance once more,
Listening in their doom for Saturn's voice.
But one of the whole eagle-brood still keeps
His sovereignty, and rule, and majesty:
Blazing Hyperion on his orbed fire   15
Still sits, still snuffs the incense teeming up
From Man to the Sun's God — yet insecure.
For as upon the earth dire prodigies
Fright and perplex, so also shudders he;
Not at dog's howl or gloom-bird's hated screech,   20
Or the familiar visiting of one
Upon the first toll of his passing bell.

---

18 drear H^1; dire $H.^2$ F.

Or prophesyings of the midnight lamp;
But horrors, portioned to a giant nerve,
Make great Hyperion ache. His palace bright,   25
Bastioned with pyramids of shining gold,
And touched with shade of bronzed obelisks,
Glares a blood-red thro' all the thousand courts,
Arches, and domes, and fiery galleries;
And all its curtains of Aurorian clouds   30
Flash angerly: when he would taste the wreaths
Of incense, breathed aloft from sacred hills,
Instead of sweets, his ample palate takes
Savour of poisonous brass and metals sick;
Wherefore when harbour'd in the sleepy West,   35
After the full completion of fair day,
For rest divine upon exalted couch,
And slumber in the arms of melody,
He paces through the pleasant hours of ease,
With strides colossal, on from hall to hall,   40
While far within each aisle and deep recess
His winged minions in close clusters stand
Amazed, and full of fear; like anxious men,
Who on a wide plain gather in sad troops,
When earthquakes jar their battlements and towers,   45
Even now where Saturn, roused from icy trance,
Goes step for step with Thea from yon woods,
Hyperion, leaving twilight in the rear,
Is sloping to the threshold of the West.
Thither we tend." Now in clear light I stood,   50

---

32 *Komma hinter* incense *u.* hills *F., fehlen H*[1,2].

Relieved from the dusk vale. Mnemosyne
Was sitting on a square-edged polish'd stone,
That in its lucid depth reflected pure
Her priestess' garments. My quick eyes ran on
From stately nave to nave, from vault to vault. 55
Through bow'rs of fragrant and enwreathed light,
And diamond-paved lustrous long arcades.
Anon rush'd by the bright Hyperion;
His flaming robes stream'd out beyond his heels,
And gave a roar as if of earthy fire. 60
That scared away the meek ethereal hours,
And made their dove-wings tremble. On he flared.

---

54 eye H^1; eyes H^2. F. 57 diamond-paved F.; diamond-paned $H^{1,2}$. *Forman weist mit Recht auf die völlige Ueber-einstimmung des Verses mit Hyp. I, 220 hin. Keats schrieb sehr gewöhnlich u für v.* 58 H^1 *hat hinter* Hyperion *ein Komma,* H^2 *gar kein Zeichen,* F. *ein Semikolon.*